The Gospel for Helpers

A 40-Day Devotional for Caring, Empathetic Supporters

BY TYLER ZACH

"A beautiful tool to support identifying your unmet needs and discover better strategies to meet your needs. Zach has woven personal stories and stories from Scripture that will help you to hear God's loving voice saying, 'I'm here with you, your pain is My pain. And I want to give you everything you need.' "

— **Tristen Collins, LPC, author of *Why Emotions Matter***

"As a 2w1 on the Enneagram, I can easily slip into a near-compulsive pattern of service, turning my faith into something that is grounded in work, not grace. It's a tough pattern to break, especially when my heart longs to help those in need. Thankfully, this book provided me with a daily reminder that I can rest in Jesus' work, rather than trying to earn a place with my own. Now that is good news."

— **Michele Cushatt, motivational speaker and author of *I Am: A 60-Day Journey to Knowing Who You Are Because of Who He Is***

" ... A personalized devotional for your personality type. I love it! ... "

— **Les Parrott, PhD, #1 *New York Times* bestselling author of *Saving Your Marriage Before It Starts***

" ... an extraordinary gift to all Enneagram enthusiasts ... "

— **Marilyn Vancil, author of *Self to Lose, Self to Find: Using the Enneagram to Uncover Your True, God-Gifted Self***

" ... Journey through these pages to remember who you are and how to bring your best self to a world in need. ... "

— **Drew Moser, PhD, author of *The Enneagram of Discernment: The Way of Vocation, Wisdom, and Practice***

" ... clear, compelling, and beyond profound."

— **John Fooshee, president of People Launching and Gospel Enneagram**

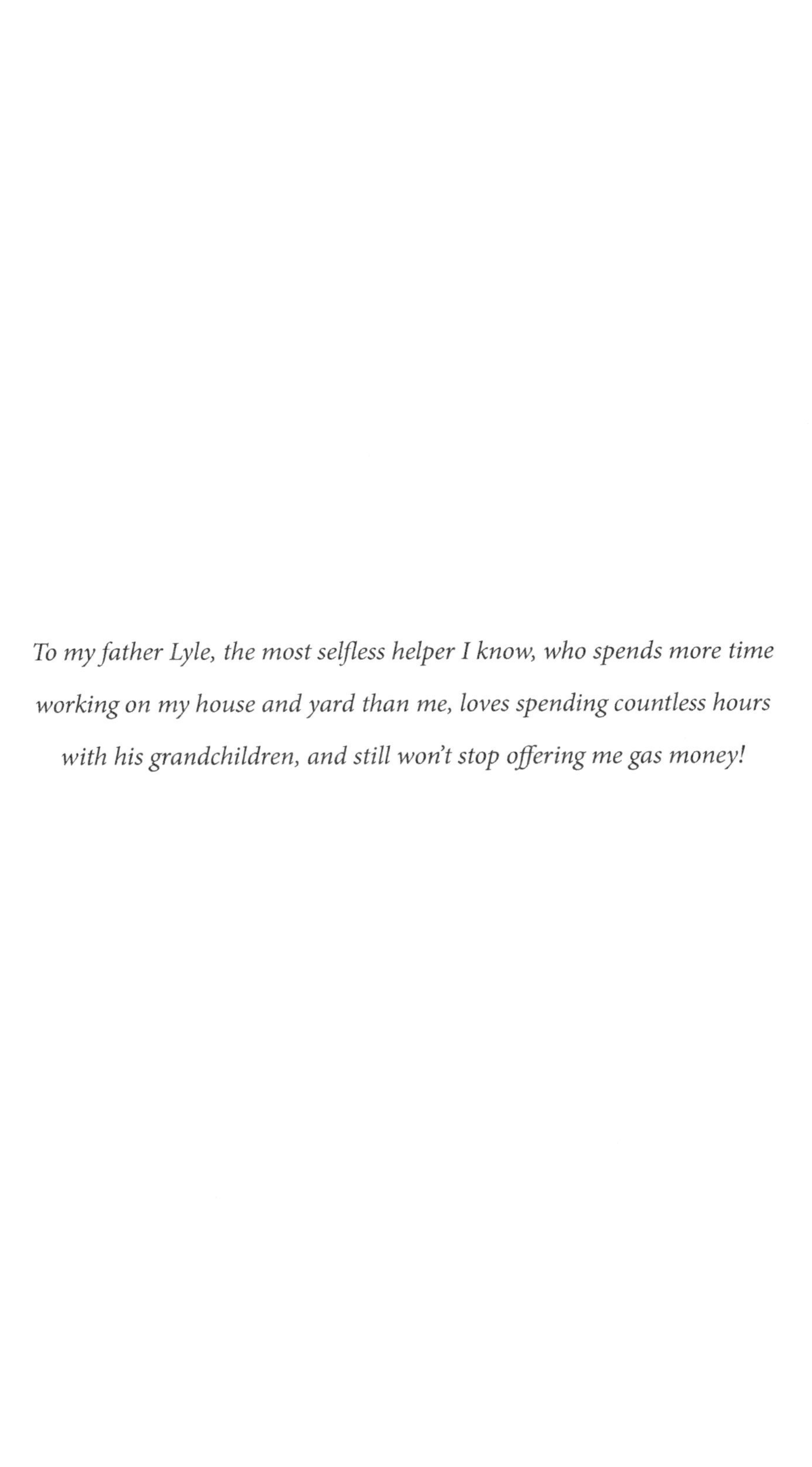

To my father Lyle, the most selfless helper I know, who spends more time working on my house and yard than me, loves spending countless hours with his grandchildren, and still won't stop offering me gas money!

Table of Contents

Foreword

WHEN JEFF AND I FIRST DISCOVERED THE Enneagram, finding books written from a Christian worldview wasn't easy. We understood how important gospel-centered Enneagram resources could be, and that inspired us to start our business, Your Enneagram Coach. Since then, we've helped over one million people find their Type through our free assessment and watched them grow through our online classes, coaching certifications, books, and podcast.

The Enneagram is a tool that clarifies our fallen nature while also reminding us we are created in the *imago Dei* (image of God). When Jeff and I understood the why behind our thoughts and actions, it transformed how we looked at ourselves, our relationships with God, our marriage, our parenting, and (obviously) our careers. Taking a risk by starting a business was both exciting and terrifying. We could have easily spun out of control or run out of gas (at times, we did!), but knowing the Enneagram as seen through the lens of the gospel kept us grounded and on track.

Our daughter, Libby, is a Type Two. She always makes sure the people around her feel well-cared for and loved. Her genuine interest in others and her ability to come alongside and help anyone in need is an inspiration to our family. We can always count on her to remember and celebrate our big life moments and make them extra special.

The world needs Type Twos because you reveal God's compassion and care. You are the relational backbone of every group. You are sensitive and empathetic to others and offer an optimistic and hands-on approach that is greatly needed in our broken world.

Like all numbers, Type Twos can have seasons of struggle. You tend to take on too much, burn yourself out, and neglect your own self-care. Deep inside, you fear that love is earned and you can only receive it through selfless service to others. The Enneagram can help you recognize this false belief and bring it to Jesus, who always loves you unconditionally, not because of your good deeds but because of who you are—His beloved child.

Type Twos, we are confident this 40-day devotional will guide you toward a more balanced you. Your needs and emotions are just as important as those you serve, and when you fill your heart with Christ's living water, you can better serve others from the overflow.

Jeff and I are thankful the Lord has provided more gospel-centered Enneagram teachers like Tyler Zach. Whether you are new to the Enneagram or have studied it for years, we know you'll find lasting value in this book. Tyler's creative wisdom shines on these pages, and his focus always remains on Jesus. We're praying that God will meet you on these pages, and you will recognize your inherent value as His beloved child.

Jesus is "the founder and perfecter of our faith."[1] He finished the great task He set out to accomplish.[2] A vital part of His ministry was to stay in alignment with His Father, and He did this by setting aside time for rest and reflection. He invites you to do the same—to come away, separate from the crowds, and be with Him. Remember, you are loved and valued for simply being you. You do not have to gain Christ's approval. You are accepted right now as you are.

—Beth and Jeff McCord
co-founders of Your Enneagram Coach
best-selling authors of *More Than Your Number: A Christ-Centered Enneagram Approach to Becoming AWARE of Your Internal World*

---

1   Hebrews 12:2

2   See John 19:30.

Introduction:
The Gospel for Helpers

You are wanted. You are generous, hospitable, empathetic, unselfish, caring, affirming, supporting, sacrificing, and nurturing. You are always thinking about others, and yes, we feel the love! But let me ask you: *Who are you when no one needs you? What if you didn't have to be needed to feel wanted?*

These are important questions because you are in higher demand than any other personality type. You are always there for us. You show up when we need you the most. At the same time, your worth doesn't come from being needed but from the One who made you. The truth we'll unpack together in this book will be challenging and freeing at the same time, but it can all be wrapped up in this one simple statement: *God doesn't need you—He wants you.* Though others may have made you feel you were loved because of your helping hands, God wants you just for being *you.*

Because God created you, He gets you! Your heavenly Father holds space for every emotion you've ever felt and expressed. Your emotions aren't too much for Him—and in fact, they make you more like Him. While Jesus represents the head, Twos are the "heart" of the body of Christ, leading us with understanding and compassion. Though expressing feelings is still frowned upon in many families and workplaces, God wants you to be brave in letting your full self be heard. He wants you to know you have what it takes to help the world "get out of our head" and live as cherished human beings, not human doings.

Over the next 40 days, I want to come alongside you to encourage your journey of making the world a more loving place and helping those who are suffering. I want to help you find freedom from the heavy burden of feeling responsible for everyone around you and redefine your idea of love to include receiving, not just giving. I want to help you find yourself in Christ rather than losing yourself in others and learn that Christ's acceptance, not man's rejection, is the measure of your worth. I want to help you love yourself as much as you love others, let go of resentment toward those who've hurt you, and fight for reciprocal relationships instead of always being the rescuer. Remember, Two, God loves you not because you are useful, but because you are His. Therefore, slow down and let this be your daily motto over the next 40 days: *God's love for me first, then relationships.*

The Enneagram can be a helpful and necessary tool for spiritual growth through self-awareness. Unlike other personality profiles, the aim of the Enneagram is to uncover why we do what we do—to help us see what lies behind our strengths and weaknesses. If we use this as a diagnostic tool, allowing the Bible to provide the language for our interpretation, then the Enneagram can produce great change in our lives, relationships, and work.

This is a book about Enneagram types, but don't be mistaken. Fundamentally, I'm a pastor who believes the Bible is the inspired Word of God and is sufficient for all He requires us to believe and do. That said, I also believe God has provided additional insights in fields like medicine and psychology that are helpful in understanding the incredible world God has made. We must tread carefully as we draw insights from fields with limited horizons of evidence like psychology. (We still have so much more to learn about the brain!) As with anything we come across in this fallible world, we can put on our gospel lens and make use of the wisdom God has poured out on the whole human race.

What Makes This Book Different?

While there are other projects explaining the Enneagram, the primary aim of this book is to go deeper by applying the truth of God's Word specifically to your type over the next 40 days. If you are suspicious of the Enneagram or know someone who is, download my free resource called *Should Christians Use The Enneagram?* at gospelforenneagram.com. I pray it will help you engage with the Enneagram as a Christian, and then talk about it with others.

Before we get to the daily devotions, let's look at how the gospel both affirms and challenges the unique characteristics of your type.

The Gospel Affirms Helpers

God sympathizes with Helpers' worldview. This selfish world lacks love in many ways, filled with thoughtless, insensitive, and unthankful people, and we need caring, supportive Helpers who will show up for others in their time of need, lead us to live sacrificially in a culture that only thinks of themselves, teach us how to be understanding and empathetic, and demonstrate how to love our neighbor as ourselves. Therefore, Helpers will be happy to know the Bible affirms the following beliefs:

• **God created us to be warm and affectionate.** "Love one another with brotherly affection. Outdo one another in showing honor."[1]

• **God created us to be selfless and caring.** "And the crowds asked him, 'What then shall we do?' And he answered them, 'Whoever has two tunics is to share with him who has none, and whoever has food is to do likewise.'"[2]

• **God created us to be generous and hospitable.** "Contribute to the needs of the saints and seek to show hospitality."[3]

• **God created us to be present and empathetic.** "Rejoice with those who rejoice, weep with those who weep."[4]

• **God created us to be kind and encouraging.** "Therefore encourage one another and build one another up, just as you are doing."[5]

• **God created us to be appreciative and thankful.** "Rejoice always, pray without ceasing, give thanks in all circumstances; for this is the will of God in Christ Jesus for you."[6]

---

1 Romans 12:10

2 Luke 3:10-11

3 Romans 12:13

4 Romans 12:15

5 1 Thessalonians 5:11

6 1 Thessalonians 5:16-18

- **God created us to alleviate pain and suffering:** "Religion that is pure and undefiled before God the Father is this: to visit orphans and widows in their affliction, and to keep oneself unstained from the world."[7]

The gospel also provides specific challenges to Helpers. Now we'll explore the most common lies Twos believe and see how the Bible provides much better promises and blessings. We will move deeper into each of these throughout the next 40 days.

- **Lie #1: I am not wanted or lovable as I am.** Twos fear that they will be rejected for being unwanted or unlovable. Therefore, they strive to present a likable, acceptable image in the eyes of others. They fall into the trap of telling themselves, "I can make people like me by being less like me" which leads to disowning the parts of themselves that are truly valuable. But keeping the mask on indefinitely will only perpetuate the lie that you are not loved for who you really are. You are the one Christ lived and died for, and with Him you never have to be someone else. He came to offer a proposal of eternal love and friendship, so you don't have to keep guessing whether you are worth pursuing or if love will ever come. You are wanted, loved, and cherished right now just as you are.

- **Lie #2: I'm only worthy of love when I'm helpful.** Twos feel a deep sense of "needing to be needed" because they think to themselves, *If you need me, you won't reject me.* But the amazing truth is that God didn't create you because He needed something from you but because He wants you. When you drift from the gospel promise that you are worthy because of Christ, you will work under the assumption, *I am needed and worthwhile because of what I can do for you.* Driven by a fear of becoming useless or replaceable, Twos will labor *for* love by helping or befriending others instead of living *from* God's love. But the truth is you are loved for whose you are, not what you do for others. Jesus died on the cross for you—for your real self, not your generous, helpful, crafted self.

- **Lie #3: I must give to get what I need.** Twos fear that if they honestly and forthrightly share their needs with others, they might be rejected and feel humiliated for asking. Therefore, to get their emotional needs met, they "give

---

7   James 1:27

to get," although this happens mostly unconsciously. They may buy gifts, give compliments, or serve others with the hope (or expectation) that others will return the favor when the time comes. Therefore, what appears to be altruistic giving comes with hidden strings attached. But Jesus, having only pure intentions, gave Himself for us expecting nothing in return. We don't have to give anything to get His ongoing favor and approval; His love is given as a free gift, not something that can be earned or exchanged for more affirmation.

- **Lie #4: I'm not enough without others.** Twos are prone to finding their identity in relationships. They find deep emotional connections—romantic and platonic—to be the juice of life. The lie Twos are led to believe is, *I'm not enough without others.* When Twos forget their perfect union with Christ, they exaggerate their need for others and will seek to merge with them, asking, "Who do they want me to be?" They may sacrifice their own needs, dreams, or freedom to gain approval and prevent rejection. But the good news is you can pile all of the deepest longings of your heart onto someone without having to make unhealthy sacrifices. When you begin a relationship with Christ, as His beloved, rather than losing yourself or becoming someone you're not, you become more of who you were created to be.

- **Lie #5: Others can't live without me.** The vice of the Two is *pride*, but not the haughty, conceited, or arrogant version that people usually think of. For the Two, pride sounds like *I will make myself so indispensable to your life (or team) that you won't be able to get along without me.* Though Twos are a beautiful reflection of God's love and care, when they forget their finiteness, they may seek to become "*The* Helper" in people's lives. But unlike the Holy Spirit, they do not have unlimited energy and resources, which may cause resentment or burnout when taking on too much responsibility for others. Pride also manifests itself through an unwillingness to ask for or receive help. Therefore, *humility*, the virtue of the Two, involves acknowledging your human limits and embracing your neediness, understanding that being a disciple of Jesus means allowing Him and others to wash your feet.

- **Lie #6: Others' needs are more important.** Average Twos find it easier to sacrifice their own needs to make others happy. When their own needs rise to the surface, the Twos' primary defense mechanism of *repression* kicks in, causing them to deny their personal needs and feelings to the point of pretending they don't have any. The lie they believe is that it is "selfish" to have needs or ask for help. But Jesus, who delights in serving you and wants you to help others without hurting yourself, desires that you fully express your needs so you can get back all that helping energy you've so generously given. Like the biblical character Martha learned, God wants you to do less standing and more sitting because you need Jesus more than Jesus needs you.

As you can see, the gospel will challenge your perception of the protagonists and antagonists in your life. In the Helper's benevolent kingdom, those who are the most affirming and sacrificial are rewarded while those who are ungrateful and self-centered are punished. Your heroes become those who boost your self-esteem, reciprocate your help, say thank you, acknowledge you, and tell you they can't live without you! Likewise, your villains become those who force you to acknowledge your limits, challenge you to slow down and rest, give you constructive criticism, reject your offers to help or spend time together, and those hard-to-please people who are not easily won over by your charisma.

God's kingdom will not be filled with those who prided themselves on being indispensable to others, but rather men and women who came helpless to the throne of grace and depended on Christ's sacrifice alone for salvation. In this place, a need to be needed is exchanged for neediness; self-denial for self-care; self-forgetfulness for self-love; codependency for healthy boundaries; and helping people become more dependent on the Holy Spirit, not you. In this place, you live for God rather than the eyes of others, learn to express your needs rather than repress them, ask for permission rather than assuming you know what others need, and receive divine courage to let some of your relationships end so that the next chapter of your life can truly begin. In this place, you can finally learn to say no to others so that you can say yes to the Shepherd's invitation to lay down in green pastures and rest beside still waters until all your needs are met.

The Invitation

When Jesus Christ, the divine all in all, entered into flawed and limited human history, He started His mission with an invitation: "The time is fulfilled, and the kingdom of God is at hand; repent and believe in the gospel."[8] He explained that to enter the good, eternally renewing life that begins well before the grave, you must do two things: believe the truth and turn from sin. Believing includes acknowledging who God is, who He says we are, and what He has done for us. More than that, to truly believe in a Christlike way is to actively live into those acknowledgments. Turning includes shedding our false worldview, misplaced desires, strong defenses, hide-and-seek strategies, and self-salvation efforts.

If you are ready to begin this incredible 40-day journey and accept God's invitation, then let's go! It will be an enlightening ride of rapid growth in the days to come as you become more self-aware and experience newfound freedom. You will encounter many aha moments as you read profound truths for your type— and maybe even learn something about the people around you. The things you learn about yourself in this book will stick with you for the rest of your life.

Three Types of Helpers

To further explore how Twos can look very different from one another, please check out the "Three Types of Helpers" in the back of this book. These "subtypes" are helpful in understanding the nuances of the Helper and will explain why some truths in this devotional will hit home more than others. These descriptions tend to err on the negative side, but they are meant to help you further uncover the unconscious motivations driving your behavior and may even help you discover why you're often confused with other Enneagram types!

---

8   Mark 1:15

You Are Wanted

For God so loved the world, that he gave his only Son, that whoever

believes in him should not perish but have eternal life.

—John 3:16

I REMEMBER GETTING DOWN ON ONE KNEE like it was yesterday. Two years prior to the engagement, I had first met my wife, Lindsey, in the Student Center on campus where she was selling candy bars to (ironically) go on a health club trip to Florida. Because she was so gorgeous, I bought not one but two candy bars to impress her. (I know, I'm a big spender.) She was, and still is, the most beautiful woman I have ever seen.

> The greatest thing you'll ever learn is just to love and be loved in return.
>
> —Eden Ahbez[1]

I proposed on our second anniversary. Recreating our very first date, I reserved a spot at our favorite Mexican restaurant, followed by a trip to a coffee shop that was closed down for the night. Because I knew the owner, he gave me the keys, allowing me to set up candles, a bottle of wine, and a projector to play the first

---

1   "Nature Boy," AZ Lyrics, accessed on September 29, 2022, https://www.azlyrics.com/lyrics/natkingcole/natureboy.html.

movie we had seen together. After the movie, a friend called me "out of nowhere" because he needed me to get something for him on campus. So I drove Lindsey back to the Student Center and led her to the spot we first met.

Just as I was about to profess my love, the limo driver showed up early, but I acted fast, hugging Lindsey, and waving him off behind her back. Then, with the hidden camera rolling in a nearby fake plant, and with my best friend and sister waiting to jump out in surprise, I got down on one knee and proposed.

Did you know that God carefully and thoughtfully planned out the perfect proposal for you? He came down from heaven to earth to prove it! He had you in mind since He knit you together in your mother's womb. You are wonderfully, thoughtfully made for the sake of being loved.[2] Your considerate mind, marvelous body, warm smile, cheerful eyes, and light-hearted laugh make your company incredibly desirable to God and others. Yes, He's aware of all your flaws, and yes, He's calling you to keep maturing. But with great affection in His voice He whispers to you: *"You are wanted and lovable just as you are."* With Him, you don't have to be anyone else or be *for* anyone else: God didn't create you because He needed something from you but because He *wants* you.

In Jesus, you are wanted and loved unconditionally.

In what is likely the most quoted verse in history, Jesus began with, "For God so loved the world." That line is so powerful because it reveals God's motivation for sending His Son: *love*. In fact, that verse's author, John, went so far as to say, "God *is* love" in his first letter to the churches.[3] You and I were not created primarily to work for a paycheck or raise children or to build bigger buildings or improve the bottom line, but to enjoy and spread God's "never stopping, never giving up, unbreaking, always and forever love."[4]

Love is just as foundational as the law of gravity—the mysterious, hidden presence undergirding all creation and holding things together. Love is not an idealistic hope reserved only for romantic comedies; it's part of our everyday lives. As an

---

2   Psalm 139:13-16

3   1 John 4:8

4   Sally Lloyd-Jones, *Loved: The Lord's Prayer* (Grand Rapids, MI: Zonderkidz, 2018), back cover.

Enneagram Type Two—a Helper—God sees that you work hard to make the world a better, more loving place—a world where everyone has someone who truly loves and cares for them.

The Good News for Helpers is that you don't have to keep guessing whether you are worth pursuing. If you've ever wondered whether you have to work to make others love you, the story of the Bible answers that question. In John's epistle we read that we love because God first loved us.[5] This means we don't have to labor *for* love by helping others or by being needed but can live *from* His love. In Jesus, you are wanted and loved unconditionally. If you've freely accepted His proposal, joining the church as His bride, He offers to always hold you dear, reminding you daily: *"I cherish you."*[6]

→ Pray

Father, thank You for sending Your Son Jesus from heaven to pursue me in love. Because Christ gave Himself up on the cross, laying down His life for me, I've been cleansed and washed of every spot the accuser might use against me to make me feel unworthy and unlovable. Help me see myself in splendor through Your eyes today: holy and without blemish.[7]

---

5   1 John 4:19

6   See Ephesians 5:29.

7   Ephesians 5:25-30

Day 1 Reflections:

How loveable do you feel today? What makes you feel less lovable?

How does it feel knowing you don't have to be needed to feel wanted?

What are you hoping to get out of the next 40 days? What would you like to ask God to do?

> ### ➜ Respond
>
> Search for, listen to, and meditate on the song "Two" from the Sleeping At Last project, Atlas: II.

The Great Rescue

And Jesus went throughout all the cities and villages, teaching in their synagogues and proclaiming the gospel of the kingdom and healing every disease and every affliction. When he saw the crowds, he had compassion for them, because they were harassed and helpless, like sheep without a shepherd.

—Matthew 9:35-36

ROB AND CHASE MOVED OUT OF THEIR cozy home and into one of Omaha's most run-down apartment complexes to build relationships with the community of Karen (Kah-Ren) refugees from Myanmar. Chase taught English fifteen hours a week out of her basement apartment and cooked large-group dinners out of her tiny kitchen. She and her husband, Rob, hosted a weekly Bible study, taught the kids how to swim (and, later, to drive), took them to doctor's

> I used to think being loved was the greatest thing to think about, but now I know love is never satisfied just thinking about it.
>
> —Bob Goff[1]

---

1 Bob Goff, *Love Does: Discover a Secretly Incredible Life in an Ordinary World* (Nashville, TN: Thomas Nelson, 2012), 17.

appointments, translated their stacks of mail, and helped troubleshoot problems related to Medicaid, car insurance, and most of all—the landlord.

Right along with their Karen friends, Rob and Chase lived through bed bug infestations, cockroaches crawling on their legs while cooking in the kitchen, and sewage leaking through the bathroom ceiling from above. Moldy drywall was not replaced by the landlord's crew but simply spray-painted over. As complaint after complaint fell on deaf ears, the couple went boldly to city council meetings to advocate with officials for their beloved, neglected family. This put pressure on the landlord to initiate improvement projects totaling over $100,000. Out of this experience, with a group of friends in our church, Rob and Chase went on to start a non-profit called Yellow Door, an organization that buys and renovates quality homes, putting Karen families on a path to become independent homeowners.

I love telling this story because it beautifully illustrates God's heart for the suffering and how far He is willing to go to rescue us. Jesus, the Son of God and Rescuer from heaven, saw suffering and embarked on the greatest rescue mission of all time. The story begins with a man being placed in the garden of Eden. Though he was surrounded by the perfection of Creation, he felt *alone*. Wouldn't you? Therefore, God said, "I will make him a helper fit for him."[2] Helper is an understatement. The Hebrew word *ēzer* quite literally translates to "help meet" and is most often used to describe God's relationship to His people.[3] That is the level of rescuing and completeness Eve's community brought to Adam.

> As a Helper, you reflect God's plan for deep human relationship, offering patient love and care.

Adam and Eve joyfully partnered with their Creator in stewarding creation and filling this world with more amazing human beings. But then it happened—or rather, it *happens*. Adam and Eve rebelled, rejecting God's advice. They believed the serpent's lie that God is uncaring and stingy—holding back the secrets of a full life—and began a pattern we all continue. We tend to *take* what will, in time,

---

2   Genesis 2:18

3   "H5828 - ʿēzer - Strong's Hebrew Lexicon (KJV)," Blue Letter Bible, accessed September 16, 2022, https://www. blueletterbible.org/lexicon/h5828/kjv/wlc/0-1/.

be *offered freely*, resulting in relational conflict between creation and Creator. The Bible describes many more relationships plagued with selfishness, manipulation, envy, and violence—starting with Adam and Eve's own boys, Cain and Abel.

Thankfully, the story doesn't end there. The Creator stepped into the narrative as Jesus, where this ongoing original sin was turned backward as Christ received both life *and* death willingly on the cross. With trust and humility, He took in the world's pain, anger, and unfaithfulness and reflected only love. Jesus didn't just come to bring help in the hereafter—He offers help in the here *and* now too. As Jesus went throughout all the cities, He ministered in word *and* deed, proclaiming *and* healing. Filled with empathy, He comforted the harassed and rescued the helpless. Now, Jesus invites *you* into His ongoing rescue efforts to relieve others from the suffering of this world. As a Helper, you reflect God's plan for deep human relationship, offering patient *love and care* when you come to our rescue—which you do, over and over again.

The Good News for Helpers is found in the words of the prophet Isaiah: "For I, the LORD your God, hold your right hand; it is I who say to you, 'Fear not, I am the one who helps you.'"[4] When you were harassed and helpless, Christ "became flesh and blood, and moved into the neighborhood";[5] filled with empathy, hearing your bleating cries, Christ left the ninety-nine to rescue you. He carries you home in His arms, attends to all your needs, and advocates on your behalf. It is this Christ who wants you to know today that He will always relentlessly pursue you.

---

4   Isaiah 41:13

5   John 1:14 MSG

→ Pray

Father, I praise You for sending Your Son Jesus on a rescue mission to find me. Because Christ laid down His life as a living sacrifice, I will offer up my body as a living sacrifice to help others in need as my spiritual act of worship.[6] Help me use my unique gifts to mobilize this generation to perform countless acts of compassion wherever they are needed.

Day 2 Reflections:

How have you supported others recently through acts of service or helpful advice?

Jesus wept over the city of Jerusalem.[7] Who have you wept over? How do your tears reveal the heart of God?

Describe a time you received comfort in suffering. Who is experiencing something similar now? How can you comfort them?

→ Respond

Like Rob and Chase, identify a person or group of people who are in need and organize your family, friends, or church to ease their burden.

6   Romans 12:1

7   Luke 19:41

The Best Friend

Greater love has no one than this, that someone lay down his life

for his friends. You are my friends if you do what I command you.

No longer do I call you servants, for the servant does not know

what his master is doing; but I have called you friends, for all that

I have heard from my Father I have made known to you.

—John 15:13-15

IN THE MOVIE *CAST AWAY*, FEDEX EXECUTIVE Chuck Noland (played by Tom Hanks) is en route to Malaysia when his plane crashes over the Pacific. Stranded on a deserted island, the isolation becomes so unbearable that Noland famously paints a human face on a volleyball and names him Wilson.[2] For him, an imaginary friend was better than none at all. We all crave human contact; we

> Ponder anew what the Almighty can do,
>
> if with his love he befriend thee.
>
> —Hymn, Praise to the Lord, the Almighty[1]

---

1 "Praise to the Lord, the Almighty," Hymntime.com, accessed on October 1, 2022, http://www.hymntime.com/tch/htm/p/t/t/l/pttlta.htm.

2 "Cast Away Plot Summary," IMDb (IMDb.com), accessed October 1, 2022, https://www.imdb.com/title/tt0162222/plotsummary.

need relationships to survive. Without them, we will go just as crazy as Chuck on a deserted island.

As Jesus was preparing to leave this earth, He told the disciples with great affection that He would no longer call them servants, but *friends,* which was the Father's heart from the beginning. God walked and talked as a friend with Adam and Eve in the garden,[3] Abraham "was called a friend of God,"[4] and we're told how "the Lord used to speak to Moses face to face, as a man speaks to his friend."[5]

God's heart is for relationships. The Trinity, with its dance of effortless giving and receiving, is a blueprint for how we are supposed to relate with each other. When you show up in our lives as the generous, self-sacrificing friend that you are, you reflect the very nature of the Triune God. For Helpers, relationships are *everything*: being with people and having a close group of friends is the most fulfilling thing in life. Twos very quickly become our best friends. They are sociable, gentle, approachable, good listeners, accepting, non-threatening, and non-judgmental. And the best thing is, you don't wait for us to come to you, but you move toward us with great intentionality.

God calls you His friend.

I can keep going! You make us feel special; you remind us that we are worth your time and that you'll be there for us no matter what. You remember our birthdays, are usually the first to celebrate our accomplishments, and have a habit of putting our needs before your own. You are not only kindhearted to your friends but also to those who are "not-yet friends"—always ready to share your life story with the stranger at the party or the person sitting next to you on an airplane.

You have no category (or tolerance) for insider/outsider behavior—just as Jesus was known as "a friend of tax collectors and sinners!"[6] It feels good having someone like you in our lives that truly believes in us and is on our side. When we are unsupported, overlooked, or marginalized by others, you become an advocate for us and show that fierce power inside of you, which is why Enneagram author

---

3   Genesis 3

4   James 2:23

5   Exodus 33:11

6   Matthew 11:19

Sarajane Case has titled the Twos "Hidden Warriors."[7] Though you have a very sweet exterior by nature, hidden inside is a tender warrior just waiting to come out. You are a force to be reckoned with.

The Good News for Helpers is that God calls you His friend. As He looks at you right now, He wants you to know He is not disappointed in you. Let me ask: Are you disappointed in yourself? To put it another way: Would you choose someone just like you to be your friend? The average Two has a nagging sense of inadequacy and may carry an unshakable conviction they aren't lovable. The reason this is a big deal is because a lack of self-love will drive you to lean too heavy on your friendships—seeking constant affirmation in others.

However, when you look into the mirror and are truly grateful for what you see, *what God sees*, then and only then can you offer the gift of healthy friendship. Becoming another's best friend first starts with loving yourself with the same intensity as God loves you.

→ Pray

Father, I praise You for being my best friend. Thank You for sending Jesus to lay down His life for me and demonstrate a greater love than the world has ever seen. I will affirm today that I am lovable in Your eyes. Help me see what You see so that I can truly love myself first.

---

7   Sarajane Case, *The Honest Enneagram: Know Your Type, Own Your Challenges, Embrace Your Growth* (Kansas City, MO: Andrews McMeel Publishing, 2020), 54.

Day 3 Reflections:

Who has been a best friend to you? What do you appreciate about them?

Do you love who you are? How can you be a better friend to yourself?

How do you picture the way God is looking at you at this very moment? Is He delighted or disappointed?

> **→ Respond**
>
> This may be a little uncomfortable, but ask a friend to share what they like about you. If it helps, tell them it's an assignment!

The Helper

So God created man in his own image, in the image of God

he created him; male and female he created them.

—Genesis 1:27

DO YOU REALIZE THAT OTHERS CAN SEE God more clearly through your personality? God created all of us as "mirrors," reflecting different aspects of His heart and character to a broken, hurting world. We are truly the *imago Dei*, translating the infinite, invisible One for a finite, visible world. When walking in the Spirit, you are nurturing, generous, attentive, compassionate, hospitable, sensitive, unselfish, benevolent, affirming, supportive, and openhearted.

> We are each of us like a small mirror in which God searches for His reflection.
>
> –St. John Vianney

Pause for a moment and read that list again. You are a remarkable reflection of God's unconditional love and care.[1]

But as you know, it's impossible to reflect those characteristics of God at all times. The apostle Paul says the mirror was cracked from top to

---

1   Marilyn Vancil, *Self to Lose Self to Find: Using the Enneagram to Uncover Your True, God-gifted Self* (New York: Convergent, 2020), 77.

bottom when we exchanged the glory of God for the glory of man.[2] And it's not even a mistake relegated to people of the past; it's something we all do still. When walking in the flesh, all those previous positive attributes turn sour, and you will find yourself being possessive, intrusive, flattering, manipulative, smothering, martyr-like, patronizing, and overly accommodating.[3]

Pause for another moment and breathe! I'm not saying you are all of those things all of the time, but this list includes the things Twos say they struggle with when they aren't keeping in step with the Spirit, and we'll touch on each of these in future devotions.

However, the beautiful thing is that you, more than any other personality type, mirror the role and function of the Holy Spirit. As Jesus was preparing to leave the earth, He comforted His disciples by saying, "And I will ask the Father, and he will give you another Helper, to be with you forever."[4] This Greek word for Helper is *paraklétos*, which describes someone who comes to another's aid—an advocate, advisor, intercessor, consoler, and comforter.[5] Doesn't that list resonate with who you are?

> Like the Holy Spirit, Twos are always on the go, displaying the power of love in action.

Because Jesus associates the Holy Spirit with the term we translate as "helper," it pushes up against the view some people have of helpers as a lower-ranking assistant—someone who merely optimizes the work of another. But the Helper— the Advocate—is not less than God the Father or God the Son, but has equal dignity and value. An advocate is one who steps in to offer presence, courage, and a voice for the lonely, the fearful, and the powerless. Likewise, you as a Two should not be reduced to an assistant but be seen as someone who is powerful enough to come alongside us and strengthen us to do what we cannot do for

---

2   Romans 1:23

3   Vancil, *Self to Lose Self to Find*, 77.

4   John 14:16

5   Strong's Greek: 3875. παράκλητος (paraklétos) — called to one's aid. Accessed September 28, 2022. https://biblehub.com/greek/3875.htm.

ourselves. Like the Holy Spirit, Twos are always on the go, displaying the power of *love in action.*

The caution for you, as you seek to be a conduit of God's care for a hurting world, is to beware seeking to be "*The* Helper" in peoples' lives. While the Holy Spirit has unlimited energy and resources and can be everywhere at the same time, you obviously do not. Sometimes you might subconsciously believe or wish you have these qualities as well. But when Twos forget their finiteness, they over-identify with their strengths and see the whole world as a customer and themselves as a full-service provider. This leads to pride, resentment, and eventually to burnout.

When you drift from the gospel promise that you are worthy because of Christ, you will work hard to present a favorable image to the world that says, "I am needed and worthwhile because of what I can do for you." When unhealthy, you become a master sculptor, picking up the chisel and carving the perfect "helpful" persona for others to admire, handing over your God-given need for acceptance to people rather than God.

But it'll never be enough.

The Good News for Helpers is Jesus died on the cross for you—for your flawed self, not your generous, helpful, crafted self. You are not worthy because of your kindness, selflessness, empathy, or how much you sacrifice for others. You are, right now without any effort, the *imago Dei*. The Holy Spirit is working like a master sculptor to clear away the excess marble and reveal what God sees underneath the image you work so hard to present to others. The Creator and Sustainer of all loves you still. When He looks in your mirror, He sees the image of His Son reflected back and says, "with you I am well pleased."[6]

---

6 Mark 1:11

→ Pray

Father, I spend so much of my day fixated on how others see me rather than how You see me. Cleanse my heart of every inclination to steal the glory You deserve when I try to be the Holy Spirit in people's lives to gain their approval. Remind me that Your Son's death is proof that I don't need to pursue any other acceptance than Yours, which You already gave.

Day 4 Reflections:

Which words in the list from the first paragraph reflect the image of God in you?

When did you start to believe the lie "I'm worthy of love when others see me as kind, generous, and helpful?" What people or life experiences have reinforced that belief?

How would your life change if you found your worth in Jesus helping you rather than you helping others?

→ Respond

Write out all the reasons God loves you without listing anything you've done for others.

The Spell of Shame

So when the woman saw that the tree was good for food, and that it was a delight to the eyes, and that the tree was to be desired to make one wise, she took of its fruit and ate, and she also gave some to her husband who was with her, and he ate. Then the eyes of both were opened, and they knew that they were naked. And they sewed fig leaves together and made themselves loincloths.

—Genesis 3:6-7

> If we can share our story with someone who responds with empathy and understanding, shame can't survive.
>
> —Brené Brown[1]

SHAME IS AN EMOTION HELPERS ARE ALMOST always feeling but never let anyone see. While some personalities cannot hide their shame, Helpers have the ability to appear positive in all situations—not because they are, but because they don't want their inner-sadness or felt needs to be a burden on anyone.

We all have an Accuser within us, an Enemy who shows up whenever we fail to bring

---

1 Brené Brown, *Daring Greatly: How the Courage to Be Vulnerable Transforms the Way We Live, Love, Parent, and Lead* (United Kingdom: Penguin Books Limited, 2012), p.75.

condemnation through others' voices or even our own. Someone who steps in to tell us we are unlikable or unlovable; that our separation from the One who loves us is an impossible chasm to cross. This Accuser dwells within each of us, biding his time until distractions fall away and we are vulnerable to his lies. As tennis great Andre Agassi shared, "I've been cheered by thousands, booed by thousands, but nothing feels as bad as the booing inside your own head during those ten minutes before you fall asleep."[2]

What do you do when shame creeps in? When the distractions and feelings of accomplishment fade and you're left alone with your Accuser? After eating the forbidden fruit, Adam and Eve sewed fig leaves to cover the awful feeling of being naked and ashamed. It's an unpleasant feeling for everyone, but particularly unbearable for Helpers.

To protect themselves from the humiliation of being overlooked, taken for granted, or invisible, Twos attempt to craft the perfect persona—helpful, thoughtful, considerate, responsive, generous, caring, nurturing, supportive, self-sacrificing, empathetic, hospitable, and sensitive. They avoid at all costs looking selfish, needy, useless, inattentive, angry, self-absorbed, indifferent, stingy, or inconsiderate, so they sew their own fig leaves, a self-made image of selflessness for the purpose of self-protection.[3]

> Twos sew their own fig leaves, a self-made image of selflessness for the purpose of self-protection.

In doing so, it's almost as if the Two is saying, "I love you and you need me, therefore you won't reject me."[4] Or, put another way, "I am worthwhile because of what I can give to you and because of the care I can show you. I am needed, therefore I am. You will like me because I am generous and solicitous towards you."[5] But none of these concealments ever actually get rid of the shame that

---

2   Andre Agassi, *Open* (New York, NY: Knopf Doubleday Publishing Group, 2009), 272.

3   Scott Loughrige, Clare M. Loughrige, Douglas A. Calhoun, and Adele Ahlberg Calhoun, *Spiritual Rhythms For The Enneagram: A Handbook for Harmony and Transformation* (Downers Grove, IL: InterVarsity Press, 2019), 76.

4   Jerome Peter Wagner, *Nine Lenses on the World: The Enneagram Perspective* (Evanston, IL: NineLens Press, 2010), 37.

5   Ibid., 204.

follows us everywhere we go—no matter what fig leaves we try putting between ourselves and the feeling.

How do we break the spiral?

When Adam and Eve were naked in shame, God mercifully pursued them and replaced their fragile fig leaves with better garments. They were completely unable to break the spell of shame on their own or even come to God for help in their failure. But God came to them, making the necessary sacrifice to cover them in His mercy, just as the prodigal son's father met him on the road and covered him with grace and mercy.

The Good News for Helpers is that we are not alone. Jesus knows the creeping voice of the Accuser. Our innocent Savior took our place on the cross and was publicly humiliated. The cross was intended to shame Him, but Jesus turned the narrative on its head. He despised the shame of the cross and made a spectacle of the Accuser's powerlessness in the light of God's love and mercy. The spell is broken and the voice of shame has been defeated.

→ Pray

Father, I am ashamed about so much, but I praise You today for drawing near to me when I feel unworthy. You sent Jesus to defeat shame and free me from it. By the power of the Holy Spirit, help me to no longer feel the need to hide myself from You or others, and help me to be exactly who You've made me to be. Amen.

Day 5 Reflections:

Like Adam and Eve, how have you experienced feelings of sadness or humiliation in relationships?

What fig leaves have you worn to protect yourself from abandonment? How have you tried to "be" someone else to get someone to like you?

How has God helped you overcome the Accuser's lies that you are worthless or unlovable?

> ### ➜ Respond
>
> Today, reveal an experience of shame or humiliation to a safe person who can speak God's grace over you.

Using Your Gifts

I am reminded of your sincere faith, a faith that dwelt first in your

grandmother Lois and your mother Eunice and now, I am sure, dwells

in you as well. For this reason I remind you to fan into flame the gift

of God, which is in you through the laying on of my hands, for God

gave us a spirit not of fear but of power and love and self-control.

—2 Timothy 1:5-7

IF YOU'VE EVER BEEN CAMPING, YOU'RE PROBABLY accustomed to starting fires (or watching your outdoorsy friend do it). Dried leaves or shavings are laid down as kindling, followed by twigs, then increasingly larger sticks, and finally, logs. Once the fire's ablaze, you can then get to the good part—sitting under the stars and soaking up a good conversation. Yet all too soon, the once-roaring flames begin to die, but rather than starting the process all over

> Twos can move mountains to help their allies be successful in the things they do.
>
> –Beatrice Chestnut[1]

---

1 Beatrice Chestnut, *The 9 Types of Leadership: Mastering the Art of People in the 21st Century Workplace* (Franklin, TN: Post Hill Press, 2017), 86.

again, you just need to bend down, add fuel, and blow on the glowing embers, and they will once again burst into flame.

In his second letter to young Timothy, the apostle Paul challenged his son in the faith not to let his fire die. Paul exhorted Timothy to "fan" the flame so that his gifts were fully activated, providing light and heat for the church. Paul was concerned that his protégé could—as we all do occassionally—become complacent, allowing his presence and contributions to become cold and lethargic. Timothy's situation is unique in the New Testament as he is the first known "second generation" Christian leader, having been introduced to the gospel by his faithful mother and grandmother.

You might be asking, "What would it look like for me to 'fan into flame the gift of God'?" Helpers have a sixth sense about what other people are feeling. When they walk into a room, they are the first to intuit who is having a bad day, who is anxious, who just had a fight with their spouse, and who needs a hug. They are excellent listeners and master empathizers; usually the first person to lend you a shoulder to cry on, open up their home as a place of refuge for you, and stand by in your time of greatest difficulty. Twos are the first to follow Paul's maxim to "rejoice with those who rejoice, weep with those who weep."[2]

> You, as a Two, often know what others need before they do.

More than anyone, Twos live out Jesus' words, "It is more blessed to give than to receive."[3] They are crazy generous and always have something to give, whether it's a physical gift or a word of encouragement. Twos also have a radar that is constantly scanning their surroundings and looking for opportunities to help. My father, the most sacrificial Two in my life, will come over to my house and do projects I hadn't thought about or show up at the church I pastor and do much-needed landscaping work for hours without anyone having to ask. You, as a Two, often know what others need before they do.

Twos will go to the greatest lengths to support their families, friends, and teammates whether it means staying up all night, giving someone financial help,

---

2   Romans 12:15

3   Acts 20:35

or driving across town during an emergency. I remember receiving a call during a staff meeting from our intern: she had just been in a car wreck and was stranded. While the rest of us were discussing how to help her call for roadside assistance, our other intern and Type Two, Arian, was already up and out the door on the way to rescue her. That's just what Twos do.

The Good News for Helpers is that Christ's love inflames your capacity to be loving, caring, hospitable, sacrificial, generous, and empathetic. Your natural gifts are part of a grand plan to restore humanity, mirroring Christ's sacrificial work on the cross. Before Paul commanded us to "offer your bodies as a living sacrifice"[4] in service of God and others, Christ already demonstrated this by serving until He literally had nothing left to give—offering up His body as a gift for all humankind. We can't outgive or out serve Jesus.

Remember, you didn't start the fire, so you can't put it out! Just as the disciples on the road to Emmaus exclaimed that their hearts were burning after being with Jesus, so too have our hearts been ignited by the Holy Spirit and kept ablaze by walking with Jesus. Our only job is to keep fanning the flame!

→ Pray

Father, I wouldn't be here without You or the friends and family who have invested in me. Thank You for giving me faithful people who have prayed for, taught, disciplined, modeled for, and led me. Help me walk slowly through this world and be a holy and sacrificial presence, pouring out the fire of Your love on a world that's often careless and indifferent.

---

4   Romans 12:1 NIV

Day 6 Reflections:

Paul asked Timothy to take inventory of the spiritual deposit made by his mother and grandmother. What spiritual truths and gifts have been passed down to you from your family and/or mentors?

Which of the strengths above have been affirmed the most throughout your life?

What's one thing you can do to ignite and develop your gifts?

> **➜ Respond**
>
> Identify your strengths and give examples of how you are already using them.

Living for Others' Eyes

And when he came up out of the water, immediately he saw the heavens

being torn open and the Spirit descending on him like a dove. And a voice

came from heaven, "You are my beloved Son; with you I am well pleased."

—Mark 1:10-11

WOULD YOU DO SOMETHING YOU DON'T LIKE in order to be loved? Andre Agassi, one of the greatest tennis players of all time, said, "I play tennis for a living even though I hate tennis, hate it with a dark and secret passion and always have."[2] In his autobiography, *Open*, he spoke of a father who was unable to "tell the difference between loving me and loving tennis."[3] After winning his first Grand Slam title at Wimbledon in 1992, his father's first response was, "You had no business losing that fourth set."[4]

> If you live for people's acceptance you will die from their rejection.
>
> —Lecrae[1]

---

1 "If You Live for People's Acceptance You Will Die From Their Rejection," accessed October 5, 2022, https://goodmenproject.com/guy-talk/if-you-live-for-peoples-acceptance-you-will-die-from-their-rejection-cmtt/.

2 Agassi, *Open*, 3.

3 Ibid., 202.

4 Ibid., 165.

What drove Agassi to succeed was not a love for tennis but a desire to win the love of his hard-to-please father. Much like the tennis legend, Helpers will do almost anything to secure the sense of appreciation they so crave, to hear the words "What would I do without you?"—even if the person or people to whom they've given this power will never offer complete and lasting acceptance.

For Twos, Threes, and Fours (known as the Heart Triad), beneath the surface is an underlying fear that they are without intrinsic value. Therefore, all three of these types believe they must do something extraordinary to avoid worthlessness and to win the love and acceptance of others.[5]

When their faces are turned away from God, other-referencing Twos define themselves through the eyes of others. Whereas Threes tend to find their identity in work and Fours in their uniqueness, Twos find their identity in relationships.[6] To get their needs met, the lie Twos believe is that they must be liked by as many people as possible. This puts them on a treadmill of turning on the charm, people pleasing, flattery, or creating rapport to win others over. They shift their focus of attention away from their own feelings and needs toward others'. *Appreciation* is the oxygen that keeps them running—until the appreciation runs out—and then, burnout.

> The Lord your God is rejoicing over you with loud singing.

Enneagram teacher Helen Palmer explains, "Young Twos have a hard time being alone long enough to define themselves. They take pride in being popular with different social circles—student leaders, rebels, jocks, frats, nerds. The orientation is toward approval and away from rejection. Rejection can be devastating. If you don't get a response from someone you care about, it gets urgent inside. Rejection feels like losing your identity. 'Who will I be without you?' 'I may never feel this way again.' You stand to lose a big piece of yourself when you're rejected, when the way that you know yourself is through the eyes of others."[7]

---

5   Don Richard Riso and Russ Hudson, *The Wisdom of the Enneagram: The Complete Guide to Psychological and Spiritual Growth for the Nine Personality Types* (New York, NY: Bantam Books, 1999), 127.

6   Helen Palmer, *The Enneagram in Love and Work: Understanding Your Intimate and Business Relationships* (New York, NY: HarperOne, 2010), 65-66.

7   Ibid., 75.

Twos can feel like balloons sometimes, whose esteem is either inflated by the affirming words of others or deflated by negative (or absent) words. However, when we become dependent on others, giving them the power to extend or withhold our fluctuating self-worth—we will never find rest, even in our greatest accomplishments.

The Good News for Helpers is that our ultimate worth is held in the One who made us—and it is something that's given as a gift, not earned. Before Jesus started His ministry—the skies opened at His baptism and the affirming voice of the Father reminded Him of His value. We, too, in our baptism, hear the same life-altering words, "You are my beloved [child]; with you I am well pleased."[8] Just as a parent holds their newborn child in the delivery room in a gaze of sheer delight before the child has done anything worthy of love, so the Father gazes at you, exactly as you are. Right now, the Lord your God is rejoicing over you with loud singing.[9]

→ Pray

Father, remind me that the unconditional love I'm searching for comes from above, not from others. Help me to look upward, not outward. Your approval of me is secure because of Jesus' work to adopt me as Your beloved child. Forgive me for trying so hard to earn from others the love You've freely given. Today, I will rest in the song You are singing over me with gladness.

---

8   Mark 1:11

9   Zephaniah 3:17

Day 7 Reflections:

How does the desire for affirmation and approval manifest itself in your life?

Who are you without the validation of others? Who are you when no one needs you?

What can you do to pour the same level of encouragement you give to others right back into your own soul?

➜ Respond

Choose some affirming Scriptures to place on your desk or around your home to remind you that God is crazy about you.

You and Martha

For in six days the Lord made heaven and earth, the sea, and

all that is in them, and rested on the seventh day. Therefore

the Lord blessed the Sabbath day and made it holy.

—Exodus 20:11

JESUS ENTERED A VILLAGE AND WAS WELCOMED into the house of His dear friends, Martha and her sister Mary. In first-century Israel (and much of the Eastern world), people were judged by their hospitality, so Martha wanted to make sure she did everything possible to make Jesus feel comfortable and prepare a meal He wouldn't forget.

> Action and contemplation are very close companions; they live together in one house on equal terms.
>
> –Bernard of Clairvaux[1]

While Martha's sister Mary was sitting at Jesus' feet talking with Him, Martha became "distracted by all the preparations that had to be made."[2] Do you sometimes

---

1   Albert Haase OFM, *Saying Yes: Discovering and Responding to God's Will in Your Life* (Brewster, MA: Paraclete Press, 2016).

2   Luke 10:40 NIV

get distracted by all the tasks you need to complete? All it took was one glance at Mary, just sitting there oblivious to all the work that needed to be done, for the elder sister to start brooding. Like Martha, don't you find it frustrating when other people need to be told how to help rather than just knowing? Furthermore, Martha probably began wondering why all of Jesus' attention was fixed on Mary—why wasn't He acknowledging and appreciating all Martha was doing for Him?

Finally, Martha couldn't hold it in anymore and like a Two moving to an unhealthy Eight, she let out an angry outburst: "Lord, do you not care that my sister has left me to serve alone? Tell her then to help me."[3] It's funny—Martha telling *Jesus* what to do. Even so, Jesus graciously replied, "Martha, Martha, you are anxious and troubled about many things, but one thing is necessary."[4] In that moment, Martha let her task list trump building a heartfelt relationship with her Lord. It's something that happens to all of us. We sit down to read our Bible or pray only to jump back up because we remembered we forgot to unload the dishes or text that friend back who asked us to do something.

This often-told story props up Mary as the hero—the calm, meditative one sitting at Jesus' feet. She was even complimented while her sister was lightly rebuked. But Martha doesn't get enough credit: after all, *she* opened up her home to Jesus, not Mary! Jesus was pleased with Martha's attempt to do her absolute best to serve her Lord and put her love into action. Like Martha, God sees the big heart behind all the thoughtful things you do every day and loves how you embody the incarnation through loving service. His wisdom for you is not to stop helping entirely but to do what is only yours to do and rest at His feet.

> You need Jesus more than Jesus needs you.

Reflect on this truth: *You need Jesus more than Jesus needs you.* Do you ever ask yourself if you are doing *more* than Jesus has asked you to do? That what He may be asking you to do today is less standing and more sitting? Pastor AJ Sherrill says Twos would do well to practice Centering Prayer[5] which "is a form

---

3   Luke 10:40

4   Luke 10:41-42

5   Centering prayer has been used throughout the centuries and has been revitalized in recent decades by Thomas Keating, a Trappist monk in Snowmass, Colorado.

of stillness that prioritizes *being* over *doing*. It demands that the disciple simply show up before God and surrender any urge for performance, action, or doing."[6]

God knew what He was doing when He gave the command to rest, when He initiated the cycle in the act of creation itself. Life is intended to have cycles: we work, and then we rest and trust that the world will keep spinning even if we stop. This is not easy; society idolizes overwork. Most will look down on you if you are caught stealing, but laboring on the Sabbath is a sign of work ethic and commitment!

The Good News for Helpers is that Jesus has redeemed us from being "human doings," just as God redeemed the Israelites from being slaves in Egypt. The taskmaster's voice has been silenced, replaced with the voice that simply calls you to *be*, saying, "Come to me, all who labor and are heavy laden, and I will give you rest."[7] In the presence of Him who says, "For my yoke is easy, and my burden is light,"[8] you are reminded that your worth and value doesn't come from lightening others' burdens. No, you are loved for *whose* you are, not *what* you do for others.

→ Pray

Father, You never sleep or slumber. Remind me that the world will keep spinning if I come and sit at Your feet. Forgive me for forgetting that I am in Your image, an image in need of Sabbath rest. Help me to let go of any resentment toward the "lazy" Marys in my life who teach me by their example how to prioritize relationships over tasks.

---

6   A. J. Sherrill, *The Enneagram for Spiritual Formation: How Knowing Ourselves Can Make Us More Like Jesus* (Grand Rapids, MI: Baker Publishing Group), 75.

7   Matthew 11:28

8   Matthew 11:30

Day 8 Reflections:

When have you spent a season (or seasons) frantically helping others? How does serving others keep you from authentically connecting with them?

How did Jesus slow down to be fully present with the Father and others? Why is slowing down such an important piece of truly being present?"

What do you fear would happen if you took extended time off to rest? How might remembering that God never sleeps help your struggle?

→ Respond

Make space to be with Jesus and let Him serve you so that you aren't pouring from an empty cup.

Repressing Your Needs

And my God will supply every need of yours according

to his riches in glory in Christ Jesus.

—Philippians 4:19

ONCE UPON A TIME THERE WAS A boy who loved a tree. As he grew up, he visited her often and she came to love him as well. First, he innocently played in her shade and ate her fruit, but later, she offered her apples so he could sell them for a profit. Then, after being gone a long time, he returned (much to the tree's joy), only to remove her branches so he could build a house. Again, much later, he returned to chop down her trunk so he could build a boat. The boy's life was changed by the generosity of his friend, but by the end of the story, his friend was nothing but a stump—she had nothing left to offer and his face was one of exhaustion and disappointment.

> Come, Boy, come and climb up my trunk and swing from my branches and eat apples and play in my shade and be happy.
>
> *–The Giving Tree* by Shel Silverstein[1]

---

1 Shel Silverstein, *The Giving Tree* (New York: Harper & Row, 1964).

In a New York Times parenting article, Adam and Allison Grant reveal that they don't see Shel Silverstein's classic book *The Giving Tree* as a heartwarming story about generosity but unhealthy self-sacrifice. There's a big difference, they say, between generosity and selflessness—giving until there's nothing left of you. The Grants explain that this kind of self-sacrifice without self-care or boundaries is not sustainable: "Research shows that people who care about others and neglect themselves are more likely to become anxious and depressed. They're also less effective: When teachers give up their nights and weekends to help individual students, their classes do significantly worse on standardized tests. Similarly, selfless students see their grades falter—they're so busy solving their friends' problems that they skip their own classes and fail to study for their own exams. Self-sacrifice is a risk factor for burnout and declining productivity."[2]

Why are Twos so susceptible to helping others until there's nothing left of them? The defense mechanism of Twos is repression of personal needs and feelings. To gain their unconscious desire of being a selfless helper needed by all, they will repress their own needs and feelings to the point of pretending they don't have any. Or, if they become aware of their needs, they won't know how to communicate them, which is its own form of inner-torture.[3] Enneagram expert Beatrice Chestnut teaches that repression is a strategic defense against the humiliation of having to acknowledge neediness. It's also a survival strategy that makes the Two double down on serving with the hope others will finally see their needs.[4]

Like the Giving Tree, you may trick yourself into thinking that altruistic self-sacrifice will cover your own deficits, but it won't. The solution to repression is *expression*—naming and clearly articulating your needs to others so that the

---

2   Adam Grant and Allison Sweet Grant, "We Need to Talk about 'The Giving Tree'," The New York Times (The New York Times, April 15, 2020), https://www.nytimes.com/2020/04/15/parenting/we-need-to-talk-about-the-giving-tree.html.

3   Drew Moser, *The Enneagram of Discernment: The Way of Vocation, Wisdom, and Practice* (Beaver Falls, PA: Falls City Press, 2020), 237.

4   Beatrice Chestnut, *The Complete Enneagram: 27 Paths to Greater Self-Knowledge* (Berkeley, CA: She Writes Press, 2013).

world can give back all the helping energy you put into it. Broadcasting your needs may sound like death but remember, to have needs is to be perfectly human. To be well-functioning, healthy organs that nurture others in the body of Christ, we must not say to other Christians, "I have no need of you"[5] but humbly receive their loving support.

I know this is easier said than done. You tend to know what other people need before you know what you need. It's extremely difficult for Twos to answer the question, "What do *you* need?" as they will often respond with a blank look. Therefore, your growth path is to become keenly aware of your needs (perhaps by tracking them in a journal) and communicate them as directly as you can. Don't expect others to practice mind reading or develop a supernatural sixth sense. Just tell them what you need!

The Good News for Helpers is our generous God is eager to supply every need on one condition: *you ask*. Jesus Himself promises, "ask, and it will be given to you."[6] He goes on to make His case: "What father among you, if his son asks for a fish, will instead of a fish give him a serpent; or if he asks for an egg, will give him a scorpion? If you then, who are evil, know how to give good gifts to your children, how much more will the heavenly Father give the Holy Spirit to those who ask him!"[7]

Consider what could happen in your life if you developed a ministry of *asking* alongside your ministry of serving. Imagine how differently *The Giving Tree* story could have ended if the tree had been open and honest about her needs! Perhaps she would have had more left and the boy would have found fullness in giving, rather than expending himself and others until everything he once loved was gone. Today, when you find yourself quick to offer someone one of your branches without any hesitation; stop, reflect, and ask yourself if *you* need anything first.

---

5   1 Corinthians 12:21

6   Luke 11:9

7   Luke 11:11-13

→ Pray

Father, thank You for creating me with a heart to lavish Your generosity on the world. I enjoy that aspect of who I am. But I admit that I've helped others at great cost to my own wellbeing. Help me value my own needs as much as I value others'. Give me the courage to ask for help, not depriving others the opportunity to tangibly demonstrate their love for me.

Day 9 Reflections:

How do you identify with The Giving Tree? Do you feel like there's almost "nothing left of you" in certain relationships?

What's stopping you from asking for help? Why is it so hard?

What do you need today? Who is one person you can ask for help from today?

→ Respond

Instead of dropping hints hoping others will notice, be very direct today about something you need. Observe how good it feels to be completely honest and receive help in the moment.

Day 10:

Codependency

A man of great wrath will pay the penalty, for if you

deliver him, you will only have to do it again.

—Proverbs 19:19

ONE REASON WE APPRECIATE YOU IS BECAUSE you check off so many well-loved verses on a daily basis such as "Each of you should look not only to your own interests but also to the interests of others"[1] and of course, the most popular Biblical mantra for Twos: "It is more blessed to give than to receive."[2] No one demonstrates this better than a Two, but we must keep in mind that Jesus said those words largely to a world full of takers. Giving Twos must hear the verse in a slightly nuanced way: "It is more blessed to give *and* to receive."

> Givers need to set limits because takers rarely do.
>
> –Henry Ford

The Giving Tree, which we touched on yesterday, has become somewhat of a religious symbol of altruistic giving or even of the selfless love of Christ. Since

---

1 Philippians 2:4

2 Acts 20:35

its first publication in 1964, many Sunday school discussions and sermons have been heard about this famous Tree. But when asked about the big idea behind his classic story, author Shel Silverstein said, "It's just a relationship between two people; one gives and the other takes."[3] In other words, it's a one-sided relationship. As Adam and Allison Grant, in the New York Times article mentioned yesterday, point out, "That's not love; it's abuse."[4]

True generosity is *helping others without hurting yourself.* It's also putting a stop to your help when it turns into enabling unhealthy behaviors—like the boy's growing comfortability in *taking.* King Solomon, in his wisdom literature, warns us to not rescue someone over and over again if we want to break the unhealthy cycle.[5] It may be necessary to let people fall on their faces sometimes if it's the only way to get them to stand on their own two feet, but even that activates the great fear for Twos: once they help someone stand on their own two feet they'll say, "I don't need you anymore and walk away."

Some warning signs of this tendency for codependency include: anxiousness when you are apart, fear of abandonment, gaining self-esteem from solving the other people's problems, an inability to say no without feeling guilty, enduring mistreatment, lack of or inability to set clear boundaries, foregoing your own hobbies or interests because of the relationship, or enabling any other kind of dysfunctional behavior. Conversely, a healthy *interdependent* relationship will include feeling 100 percent safe to be fully honest, personal responsibility, feeling free and uninhibited, and not relying on each other for personal happiness.

> True generosity is helping others without hurting yourself.

Twos may unintentionally create codependent relationships when they seek out needy or dependent people from the very beginning who they believe won't abandon them. Or these relationships may develop over time when Twos

---

3   Richard R. Lingeman, "The Third Mr. Silverstein," The New York Times (The New York Times, April 30, 1978), https://www.nytimes.com/1978/04/30/archives/the-third-mr-silverstein.html.

4   Adam Grant and Allison Sweet Grant, "We Need to Talk about 'The Giving Tree'," The New York Times (The New York Times, April 15, 2020), https://www.nytimes.com/2020/04/15/parenting/we-need-to-talk-about-the-giving-tree.html.

5   Proverbs 19:19

start saying yes to small projects and then can't say no to larger ones. But once a Two is in constant demand day and night, they begin to feel overburdened and overwhelmed. Suzanne Stabile points out, "[Twos] volunteer easily, but the satisfaction of giving wears off when the expectations from others outweigh the gratitude Twos receive."[6] At this point, they begin to crave independence, wishing that people would leave them alone and go take care of themselves!

Therefore, the growth path for a Two involves getting off the swinging pendulum of dependence and independence, and pursuing healthy, give-and-take, reciprocal relationships with good boundaries. Clinical psychologist Jerome Wagner says a mature Two is someone who has gone through the dependence of childhood and the exaggerated independence of adolescence to achieve the interdependence of adulthood.[7]

Seek to empower rather than enable others, teaching them how to live independent of you. Rescuing people will rob them of the dignity and self-esteem that comes with learning how to solve their own problems. This will keep you from getting resentful of their demands and them of getting resentful toward you for treating them like a dependent.

The Good News for Helpers is "For freedom Christ has set us free; stand firm therefore, and do not submit again to a yoke of slavery."[8] Though you were created to meet others' needs, you were not created to be their prisoner. God did not intend for you to be in relationships that cut you down to a stump; He created you with the potential to grow into something truly magnificent, like a giant oak with thick, leafy branches extending far and wide, providing shade and a rest for a multitude of thankful people.

---

6   Suzanne Stabile, *The Path Between Us: An Enneagram Journey to Healthy Relationships* (Downers Grove, IL: InterVarsity Press, 2018), 82.

7   Wagner, *Nine Lenses on the World*, 200.

8   Galatians 5:1

→ Pray

Father, You are my Tree of Life who produces nourishing fruit and shade for healing.[9] You are a giver, not a taker. Help me to rely on You alone for all my emotional, physical, and spiritual needs. Forgive me for the times I've become codependent on someone else, looking to receive from them what You've already freely offered me.

Day 10 Reflections:

Which of the warning signs of codependency above have you seen in your life?

What is the difference between codependency and healthy interdependence?

How will you seek to help others without hurting yourself?

→ Respond

Let go of a relationship with someone who is more comfortable with taking than giving.

---

9   Revelation 22:2

Say No More

Keep your heart with all vigilance, for from it flow the springs of life.

—Proverbs 4:23

DO YOU OFTEN FIND YOURSELF OVERCOMMITTED AND spread too thin? One of the main reasons the Helper may end up in this place is because it's just so hard to tell people no. Why is saying such a small word such a big challenge? For starters, *no* means having to publicly acknowledge that you have limitations and don't have the capacity to be all things to all people. It also means having to set boundaries, and generally speaking, Helpers prefer to live in a world without relational boundaries, where they can move freely in and out of others' lives without needing to ask for permission.

> Our yes has no meaning if we never say no.
>
> —Henry Cloud[1]

In the physical world, boundaries like fences and signs are helpful because they define where our property ends and someone else's begins. Similarly, God created boundaries for our souls, as Henry Cloud teaches, boundaries define what is "me" and what is "not me"—where I end and someone else begins.

---

1 Henry Cloud, *Changes that Heal: How to Understand Your Past to Ensure a Healthier Future* (Grand Rapids, MI: Zondervan, 1996), 149.

Boundaries show us where our responsibilities lie—what we do and do not have authority over—and keep us from becoming doormats for others who would control areas of our lives they aren't a part of or don't have a say in.[2]

The best thing you can do right now to set healthy boundaries is to start saying no. As Christina Wilcox shares with Helpers:

> You're allowed to say that little word—"No." You're allowed to say, "Can I get back to you tomorrow?" You're allowed to say, "Let me think about it and I will let you know." These words often feel too risky. Maybe you fear saying it not because you're afraid you'll be replaced, but because you're afraid of the emotions that might arise when you do. But that's all the more reason why you should begin practicing saying "no." Start by saying no to small things, such as another night of having people over at your house. Saying no to reaching out to others all the time. Saying no to replying to texts or emails right away. As you work your way up to saying no to bigger things, notice how your value doesn't come from what you agreed or declined to do, but from who you are.[3]

> **Boundaries are not about selfishness but about stewardship.**

If you struggle to do this, Beatrice Chestnut suggests saying maybe on the way from yes to no. This intermediate step will buy you some time as you think about how to frame your no in the best possible way.[4] You don't have to apologize for saying no. Saying no doesn't mean you're being unloving or unhelpful; rather, it's loving yourself first so you can offer the healthiest version of yourself to others— like putting on your own oxygen mask first on a plane. There are many people in this world who see your generous heart and will come knocking, but the wisdom of Proverbs tells you to stand firm on your boundaries: "Keep your heart with all vigilance, for from it flow the springs of life."[5]

---

2   "What Are Healthy Boundaries?," Boundaries Books, accessed November 16, 2020, https://www.boundariesbooks.com/pages/what-are-healthy-boundaries.

3   Christina S. Wilcox, *Take Care of Your Type: An Enneagram Guide to Self-Care* (New York, NY: Tiller Press, 2021), 26.

4   Chestnut, *The Complete Enneagram.*

5   Proverbs 4:23

Setting boundaries may feel very selfish, but as Cloud clarifies, boundaries are not about *selfishness* but about *stewardship*.[6] Setting boundaries protects the time and resources God has given us to leverage for His glory. Who are you allowing to come into your "fence" and intrude on your time, decision-making, and priorities?

Healthy boundaries may sound like:

- "You often ask me at the last minute. I'll need more time to do what you asked."

- "I've decided I'm not going to text or email while I'm on my day off."

- "I would like to help, but I don't have the energy. I need to take some time for myself."

- "I know I told you 'yes, it's not a problem' but I've realized I don't have the bandwidth for that anymore."

The Good News for Helpers is that while we can't control others' behaviors, we can control our responses. This may frustrate them, particularly if this is a departure from business as usual in the relationship, but it will save us from their toxicity or unnecessary neediness. God did not create you with the capacity to say yes to everyone (even though you may think you can!) or to wait on them indefinitely to the detriment of your own life. Therefore, work on reversing that yes reflex today and say no more, remembering that setting boundaries will not end healthy relationships but *enhance* them.

> **→ Pray**
>
> Father, You are my rock and my safe place in times of trouble. I find refuge under the shadow of Your wings from the demands of this world. Help me to love myself as You love me by guarding my heart. As Your steward for my one life, enable me to set better boundaries. Let my yes be yes and my no be no.

---

6 "Am I Being Selfish When I Set Boundaries?," Boundaries Books, accessed November 16, 2020, https://www. boundariesbooks.com/blogs/boundaries-blog/am-i-being-selfish-when-i-set-boundaries.

Day 11 Reflections:

Where do you observe healthy boundaries in your life? Where might you need to set some healthy boundaries?

What do you fear will happen if you tell others no more often?

List some healthy emotional and physical boundaries you can set with your partner, parents/in-laws, and friends both at home and in the workplace.

> ### ➜ Respond
>
> Take a season of no—set aside a series of days or weeks on your calendar where you turn down every opportunity to serve that comes your way.[7]

---

7   Case, *The Honest Enneagram*, 65-66.

Giving to Get

And if you lend to those from whom you expect to receive, what credit

is that to you? Even sinners lend to sinners, to get back the same

amount. But love your enemies, and do good, and lend, expecting

nothing in return, and your reward will be great, and you will be sons

of the Most High, for he is kind to the ungrateful and the evil.

—Luke 6:34-35

When you give and expect a return, that's an investment. When you give and don't expect anything back, that's love.

–Anonymous

THERE WAS ONCE A YOUNG BOY WHO wanted to be friends with the little girl down the street, but she didn't pay much attention to him. So, grabbing one of his favorite toys, a little wind-up locomotive, he brought it to her house one afternoon. But just as he was about to give her the gift, he suddenly realized that this was a bribe (though he didn't yet have a vocabulary for it). Everything in him wanted to give her the toy to ensure she would like him and be his friend.[1]

---

1   Riso and Hudson, *The Wisdom of the Enneagram*, 134-135.

This childhood reflection shared in Riso and Hudson's *The Wisdom of the Enneagram* reveals the inner-struggle of all Helpers. Many Twos say they grew up believing the lie, "I must give to get." As children, they felt they were not loved for who they were but only for what they did for others—they felt the need to give gifts or serve to be liked or cared for. The tricky thing is that this largely happens on an unconscious level, leaving you completely unaware of this habit. Though others may experience "giving to get" behavior as manipulation, they may not understand Twos are just trying to get their emotional needs met; too often, they fear humiliation or rejection will be the result of honestly and forthrightly sharing their needs.

This "giving to get" behavior can look like buying someone dinner to get them to spend time with you, getting someone a gift on their birthday in the hopes they'll remember and do the same for you, or sending an affirming text hoping they'll give a response such as "You're such a good friend" or "What would I do without you?" Though some Twos have persuaded themselves that they are selfless and have nothing but pure intentions, you can start to see how their giving may come with strings attached. As a litmus test, ask yourself, "Have I felt hurt or resentful that they didn't return my call right away, throw me a birthday party, or bring me a meal when I was sick like I did for them?" If the answer is yes, your giving might not always be as "free" as you thought.

> Pause and check your motives when you feel the urge to give.

Pastor and author AJ Sherrill says one of the core narratives for Twos is the parable of the sheep and goats.[2] In the story, the people likened to goats lived completely selfishly, while the sheep are those who fed the hungry, gave drink to the thirsty, opened up a room for the homeless, clothed the naked, and visited the sick and those in prison.[3] While Twos are notorious for doing "all of the above" with huge hearts, one of the lessons of the parable is that the sheep were *unaware* of their actions; they fulfilled Jesus' command to "not let your left hand know what your right hand is doing."[4]

---

2   Sherrill, *The Enneagram for Spiritual Formation*, 89-90.

3   Matthew 25:35-36

4   Matthew 6:3

One of the most important action steps for Twos, Sherrill says, is to pause and check your motives when you feel the urge to give. Ask yourself: *Am I being generous because I want something in return?* Jesus, in the parable of the great banquet, taught, "When you give a dinner or a banquet, do not invite your friends or your brothers or your relatives or rich neighbors, lest they also invite you in return and you be repaid. But when you give a feast, invite the poor, the crippled, the lame, the blind, and you will be blessed, because they cannot repay you. For you will be repaid at the resurrection of the just."[5]

The Good News for Helpers is Jesus gave Himself for us expecting nothing in return. That's real, altruistic, unconditional love. We learn from our passage today that God is generous to the *ungrateful*—the thankless, unappreciative, and selfish—a group of people that Twos find particularly hard to love. Remember that even if your radical generosity is not reciprocated in any way, *God sees you* and promises that every act of kindness done in secret "will be repaid at the resurrection."[6]

→ Pray

Father, my mind cannot fathom the amount of kindness You show every day to the ungrateful. Thank You for loving me without any strings attached. Help me love others without expecting anything in return, especially those who don't acknowledge my sacrifices.

---

5   Luke 14:12-14

6   Luke 14:14

Day 12 Reflections:

Like the young boy, when have you realized you were "giving to get"?

How do you feel when others do not acknowledge, show thanks, or honor you for what you've done for them?

What can you do to encourage, befriend, or give to someone who cannot repay you?

> **➜ Respond**
>
> Give an anonymous gift, whether to a friend or charity, forfeiting the opportunity to have someone give back to you.

Addicted to Love

Jesus said to her, "Everyone who drinks of this water will be thirsty again,

but whoever drinks of the water that I will give him will never be thirsty

again. The water that I will give him will become in him a spring of water

welling up to eternal life." The woman said to him, "Sir, give me this

water, so that I will not be thirsty or have to come here to draw water."

—John 4:13-15

I'VE MADE A LOT OF MISTAKES IN the relationship department. In college, after ending a deep two-year relationship, I was left with a big void in my heart, and I immediately began pursuing another young woman. I went all out with this rebound: even buying a journal that reminded me of her and wrote daily, chronicling every detail of our first weeks together. But that faded quickly—after four months, I didn't feel the same about the relationship. What once was so fresh and new had suddenly lost my interest. I began to push her away,

> Might as well face it, you're addicted to love.
>
> —Robert Palmer[1]

---

1 "Addicted to Love," Lyrics.com, accessed on May 13, 2021, https://www.lyrics.com/lyric/2828967/Robert+Palmer/Addicted+To+Love.

finally offering the classic line, "It's not you; it's me." When those words left me, her face turned deathly cold and she said, "I have dated other guys who were complete jerks. But you are the worst of them all—because you led me on and made me believe you loved me."

My friend once told me I was "in love with being in love." I thought he was crazy at first, but maybe you've been told the same thing. Along with Fours, Twos are the true romantics of the Enneagram, though unlike Fours who are always searching for the ideal partner, Twos quite often seek to *become* the ideal partner, maneuvering themselves into the hearts and lives of others through generosity. Twos enjoy a good love story and fantasize about fulfilling experiences with their soulmate and find deep emotional connections—romantic and platonic—to be the juice of life. Many Helpers develop crushes quickly, having dreamed about being in a romantic relationship from an early age. When you do find someone you are attracted to, you may begin wondering (sometimes obsessively) *When will I bump into them again? Could we be a perfect match?*

Money, power, and success are okay, but none of those things hold a candle to love. In the words of Christian, the hopeless romantic protagonist in the musical *Moulin Rouge*, "Love? Love. Above all things, I believe in love. Love is like oxygen. Love is a many splendored thing. Love lifts us up where we belong. All you need is love."[2] There is an echo in his words from the Apostle Paul who exclaimed, "So now faith, hope, and love abide, these three; but the greatest of these is love."[3]

> The lie Twos are led to believe is, "I'm not enough without others."

However, for Christian (and sometimes Twos), love gets stretched outside of its proper boundaries. Psychoanalyst Karen Horney described what idealized love can become for others: "Love must and does appear as the ticket to paradise, where all woe ends: no more loneliness, no more feeling lost, guilty or unworthy … love seems to promise protection, support, affection, encouragement,

---

2   "Moulin Rouge!," Imdb.com, accessed on October 7, 2022, https://www.imdb.com/title/tt0203009/characters/nm0000191.

3   1 Corinthians 13:13

sympathy, understanding. It will give him a feeling of worth, it will give meaning to his life, it will be salvation and redemption."[4]

The lie Twos are led to believe is, "I'm not enough without others." When Twos forget their perfect union with Christ, they exaggerate their need for others and will seek to merge with them, becoming one heart and flesh in full surrender. But there's a high cost. As healthy boundaries get blurred, Twos may have to sacrifice their freedom, their true selves, and their sexuality. As it's been said, some people will give affection to get sex, but others give sex to get affection. Many Twos have fallen into the latter.

The Good News for Helpers is found in John 4, where we read about a woman who was perpetually searching for true love, maintaining the fantasy, even after five partners, that a relationship could heal everything wrong with her. Then she met Jesus by a well. Though the search left her emotionally and physically empty, this Rescuer lovingly invited her into an eternally fulfilling relationship. With the eyes of loving-kindness, He offered her an eternal spring of intimate fulfillment that no partner could provide. Through this story, we learn that we *can* pile all of the deepest longings of our hearts onto one person for ultimate fulfillment without having to make unhealthy sacrifices. When you begin a relationship with Christ, as His beloved, rather than losing yourself or becoming someone you're not, you become more of who you were created to be rather than less.

→ Pray

Father, You are a spring of living water overflowing in my heart. No matter what happens in my earthly relationships, I know You will never leave me. Thank You for giving me the ability to connect with others deeply. Remind me that I am enough in Your eyes so that I don't idealize relationships but keep love in its proper boundaries.

---

4   Karen Horney, M.D., *Neurosis and Human Growth: The Struggle toward Self-Realization* (New York: W. W. Norton & Co., 1950), 239–40.

Day 13 Reflections:

What do you appreciate about your romanticism—your love of love, words of appreciation, and gestures of affection? How have others benefited from it?

To what extent do you rely on daily emotional connections, romantic or platonic, to keep you happy?

Do you believe you are enough without others? How can you live out this truth today?

→ Respond

Write a goodbye letter to someone from your past to get closure. Include why you are saying goodbye, how it makes you feel, special memories with them, things they taught you, what you want them to know, and what you will always remember.[5]

---

5   This exercise comes from www.therapistaid.com.

Blind Spots in Love

If I give away all I have, and if I deliver up my body to be burned, but have not love, I gain nothing. Love is patient and kind; love does not envy or boast; it is not arrogant or rude. It does not insist on its own way; it is not irritable or resentful; it does not rejoice at wrongdoing, but rejoices with the truth. Love bears all things, believes all things, hopes all things, endures all things.

—1 Corinthians 13:3-7

> I want you to be happy but I want to be the reason.
>
> –Anonymous

AS I'VE MENTIONED, RELATIONSHIPS ARE EVERYTHING TO the Helper. Twos put a lot of energy into their relationships and expect others to do the same. They feel most valued when others are fully present, engaging in heart-to-heart conversation with them and because they often have trouble accessing their own feelings, they enjoy being with people who can draw them out.[1] Generally speaking, Twos are drawn to successful people who will acknowledge them and

---

1 Stephanie Barron Hall, *The Enneagram in Love: A Roadmap for Building and Strengthening Romantic Relationships* (Emeryville, CA: Rockridge Press, 2020), 33-34.

suffering people they can help. In romantic relationships, meeting emotional needs are a prerequisite for sexual intimacy—Twos prioritize emotional intimacy over all other aspects of the relationship. Though they have great emotional strength, they still desire gentleness in conflict and reassurance from their partner that the relationship is still secure.[2]

Today, we are going to look at some of the blind spots that Twos have in relationships. Though it won't be easy, the heart behind it is to help you improve relationships and avoid pain (for yourself and others) and rejection in the future. One place in Scripture that talks about blind spots in love is the apostle Paul's classic chapter on love in 1 Corinthians.

In the opening section, Paul shares that love is more than demonstrating radical generosity and sacrifices—things that come naturally for Twos. Average Twos enjoy winning others over, pulling them in, and becoming the special friend who's given access to privileged information; they thrive on being kept informed and consulted on big decisions.[3] Over time unhealthy and insecure Twos may become possessive, smothering, and feel like they have to constantly hover and check in. They must remember that real love gives others freedom: the kind of love that desires the best for others involves setting boundaries or even fully withdrawing from another's life at times—*letting go*. Love means helping others to be strong and independent, not more dependent on you.

> Love means helping others to be strong and independent, not more dependent on you.

Love does not boast. It does not continually call attention to everything you are doing for others or saying things like, "If it weren't for me, where would you be?" *Love does not insist on its own way.* Rather than listening to someone all the way through, do you sometimes stop to insert your advice? When pride puffs up, you might begin insisting that you already know what they need prematurely. *Love is not rude.* It doesn't expect others to magically read your mind as you sit and

---

2   Stephanie Barron Hall, *The Enneagram in Love: A Roadmap for Building and Strengthening Romantic Relationships* (Emeryville, CA: Rockridge Press, 2020), 36-37.

3   Riso and Hudson, *The Wisdom of the Enneagram*, 135.

wait to see if they pick up your needs by radar … which usually turns into Twos saying, "I'm tired of having to tell you what I need when you should just know!"[4] *Love is not irritable or resentful.* Twos sometimes want so much engagement that no amount feels like enough. They need to be more aware of this so they can be more forgiving when others don't come through for them the way they had hoped. (For example, "Jeff said hello and asked about my day, but if he really cared, he would have stopped and had coffee with me."[5])

These blind spots are general for Twos and may not apply to you. Either way, they aren't fun to hear, so let me remind you how much we appreciate you: you beautifully demonstrate that *love is patient and kind* as you exude benevolence, warmth, and optimism. You don't judge but receive us with open arms. Being more comfortable with affection than any other type, you are always there to give us a hug when we are down. Thank you for making things fun, being an incredible listener, emotionally attuned to our feelings, and for *always* running toward us when we are in need. Your love for us *bears all things, believes all things, hopes all things, endures all things.*

The Good News for Helpers is that in the light of Jesus' life of sacrificial love, we can see our blind spots clearly. Through Jesus, the multi-faceted love of the Triune Godhead described in 1 Corinthians 13 has been made visible to us. Just as a diverse spectrum of bright colors shine through a crystal prism, so too does the patience, kindness, truth, and enduring love of the Father shine through the Son with magnificent glory. If you have seen and tasted this radiant love, go and love others in the same way today.

---

4   Ian Morgan Cron and Suzanne Stabile, *The Road Back to You* (Downers Grove, IL: InterVarsity Press Books, 2016), 119-120.

5   Riso and Hudson, *The Wisdom of the Enneagram*, 136-137.

➜ Pray

Father, You have loved me so well. When it comes to loving others without expectations, my love sometimes falls short. Help me release any lingering possessiveness, jealousy, or resentment I have toward my loved ones. Enable me by Your Holy Spirit to offer others freedom and forgiveness from the well of Your steadfast love, which endures forever.

Day 14 Reflections:

How have you demonstrated God's love through your kindness, patience, and endurance?

Who do you need to give more freedom? How can you begin letting go of them today?

Which blind spot do you struggle with the most? What can you do about it?

➜ Respond

Identify a person you are unhappy with right now. List the unwritten expectations you have for them. Are they realistic? Try reevaluating any unrealistic expectations and re-engage with more patience.

Dealing with Rejection

He has said, "I will never leave you nor forsake you." So we can confidently

say, "The Lord is my helper; I will not fear; what can man do to me?"

—Hebrews 13:5b-6

I'VE BEEN TOLD FRIENDSHIP BREAKUPS ARE EXTREMELY painful for Helpers. Due to their heavy emphasis on relationships, they may become more vulnerable to rejection than other types, which means that dealing with rejection will probably be one of the most difficult ongoing challenges you'll face in life. A Two friend of mine told me, "Rejection is still one of my greatest fears, and one of the main reasons I spent twelve weeks doing intensive trauma-informed therapy. I had to learn not everything—even failed or broken relationships—was my fault."

> Rejection doesn't mean you aren't good enough; it means the person failed to notice what you have to offer.
>
> —Mark Amend[1]

After getting burned—even once—it can be a real challenge to trust others who profess

1   John E. Markley, *Lead Yourself Today* (Bloomington, IN: WestBow Press, 2014), 141.

their loyalty. Enneagram teacher Suzanne Stabile shares, "Twos have a hard time trusting people when they say, 'I'm not going anywhere,' or 'You can count on me if you need me.' I have always thought, *Yeah … maybe. Maybe you will be there for me.* But in my heart, I have struggled to believe I'm worth it."[2]

Living with a fear of rejection will continually drive you to offer strategic help to hold on to an important place in the lives of others. But as we discussed in Day 12, it will keep you thinking to yourself, *I must say no to my needs and yes to others or else I will be rejected.* This fear will also cause you to keep your true feelings to yourself: *If I tell them what I really feel, won't they get upset? What if they hang up, leave, or move on to someone else?*

Kahneman and Tversky's Nobel Prize-winning findings on "loss aversion" claim that the psychological pain of losing is twice as powerful as the pleasure of gaining.[3] We will burn hours and calories to keep the boat from rocking rather than risk being set adrift. Think for a moment: *Do you work harder avoiding the loss of a relationship or toward the growth and strengthening of new ones?* A fear of rejection may lead you to burn all your calories on relationships that are no longer serving you rather than find more healthy ones.

> Rejection does not determine the measure of your worth.

The growth path for Twos involves learning how to work through rejection rather than avoiding it. After all, when we signed up to follow Jesus, rejection is not a matter of *if,* but *when.* As Jesus was sending out the seventy-two to nearby towns and villages, He warned them that they would be rejected, but He followed the warning up with a promise: "The one who hears you hears me, and the one who rejects you rejects me, and the one who rejects me rejects him who sent me."[4]

Jesus came down from heaven with arms wide open but, "He came to his own, and his own people did not receive Him."[5] He lamented over the fact that His loving care was rejected: "O Jerusalem, Jerusalem … How often would I have

---

2   Stabile, *The Path Between Us*, 86.

3   "Prospect Theory: An Analysis of Decision under Risk," accessed November 18, 2020, https://www.jstor.org/stable/1914185.

4   Luke 10:16

5   John 1:11

gathered your children together as a hen gathers her brood under her wings, and you were not willing!"[6] That could very well be a life verse for Twos!

The Good News for Helpers is God knows what it feels like to be forsaken: "He was despised and rejected by men, a man of sorrows and acquainted with grief; and as one from whom men hide their faces he was despised, and we esteemed him not."[7] Pause for a moment and reflect on that verse. Is it not truly profound that the Savior you follow knows what it's like to carry immense sorrow and grief over being rejected by the people He came to love and save from their suffering? If you are still carrying grief today over your relationships, then hear this: *Jesus knows and will not forsake you.*

In Jesus' time of greatest need, His closest friends doubted, denied, deserted, or in the case of Judas—delivered Him over to death. Jesus spent His entire ministry loving, caring for, serving, and teaching … Judas. What did He get out of His investment? Not just an emotional loss but the loss of His life. We too will have Judases in our lives, so remember these words today: Rejection does not determine the measure of your worth. Just because someone rejects you doesn't mean you are not worthy of being loved.

→ Pray

Father, You know what it feels like to be rejected by those You love. Fill me so that I can love others even when they don't love me in return. Remind me that I am wanted and loved apart from what I do. Because You will never forsake me, I will confidently say, "The Lord is my helper; I will not fear; what can man do to me?"[8]

---

6   Luke 13:34

7   Isaiah 53:3

8   Hebrews 13:6

Day 15 Reflections:

Make a list of all the reasons someone might reject you. What does this list reveal about where you are finding your worth?

How might past rejection be causing you to mistrust the motives of those around you now?

With whom can you talk through and process the rejection you've experienced in a healthy way?

→ Respond

Ask God for the supernatural power to forgive those who've rejected you.

Wearing a Million Masks

But when I saw that their conduct was not in step with the truth of the gospel, I said to Cephas before them all, "If you, though a Jew, live like a Gentile and not like a Jew, how can you force the Gentiles to live like Jews?"

—Galatians 2:14

ONE OF THE HELPER'S "SUPERPOWERS" IS THE ability to pick up on the needs and feelings of others. You notice others' likes and dislikes, the colors they wear, the food they enjoy, and what makes them happy. This is what makes you a great conversationalist: if you sense they love cooking or football, you might let them know you also love those things and bring up news related to those topics to create a common connection.

> People pleasing hides the real you.
>
> –Anonymous

All Twos have a highly advanced "people radar" that picks up even the most subtle signals of others' moods and preferences. All of this data is then compiled for the purpose of image management—becoming the person others need you to be. Though this process is mostly unconscious, it is no less real. As Helen Palmer explains, "They mold themselves appropriately: 'Should I be a soft person, an aggressive person, lighthearted, or dead serious?' It's not a matter of faking it or putting on a mask; it feels more like getting along with people so that we all like one another."[1]

Twos, Threes, and Fours all have a similar identity problem: believing they are not loved for who they really are. So, all three types disown their true selves and create a specific mask to gain the approval of others. "While Threes create an image of achievement and success, and Fours present themselves as unique and special," explains Beatrice Chestnut, "Twos strive to have a likable, pleasing image."[2] The internal dialogue goes like this, "You see me and like me, therefore I exist."[3]

But what happens if they *don't* see you, or worse, don't like you?

One cost of perpetually wearing masks is the sacrifice of intimacy in those truly close relationships. Though Twos are one of the most naturally social types and make close relationships look simple, they may ironically fear intimacy ("into-me-see") because it requires full authenticity—and being fully *you* may lead to rejection. Another downside to living with masks is enduring solitary sadness underneath the happy exterior you present. You lose touch with your real self and with the truth—the truth of who you are and any truth you ought to be speaking into the lives of your close companions. You can't speak the truth in love if you only give people what they *want* to see and hear.

> You were not created to be a prisoner to the expectations of others.

In his letter to the Galatians, the apostle Paul recalled a time he called out Peter on this very issue. While in Antioch, Peter gave the Gentiles the impression he was comfortable eating with them (a sign of acceptance). However, when the more orthodox Jewish-Christian leaders showed up from Jerusalem, Peter distanced himself from the new Gentile converts, creating a rift in the fledgling community. Paul, who had worked so hard to bring these groups together, called

---

1 Palmer, *The Enneagram in Love and Work*, 66.

2 Chestnut, *The Complete Enneagram*.

3 Wagner, *Nine Lenses on the World*, 203.

out this duplicitous behavior, reminding Peter that such hypocrisy was out of step with the gospel.

Peter's experience is one of our worst fears coming true. Imagine having all of your family and friends showing up in your living room at the same time expecting you to back their likes and dislikes. We may be able to switch between two personas quickly, but we can't be both at the same time! Are you exhausted from trying to be who others want you to be? What artist Ryan O'Neal sings to Threes is also relevant for Twos: "It's so exhausting on this silver screen where I play the role of anyone but me."[4]

The Good News for Helpers is that God created you to be your redeemed self and no one else. You were not created to be a prisoner to the expectations of others. Keeping the mask on indefinitely will only perpetuate the lie that you are not loved for who you really are but for who you are for others. *You* are the one Christ lived and died for, and with Him we never have to be someone else. Today, remember that you are *more than your role*: You may find yourself identifying as a parent, teacher, caregiver, spouse, best friend, or guardian of a cause rather than who you are as an individual.[5] Take the mask off today and *just be you.*

→ Pray

Father, You created me perfect in Your image. Forgive me for the masks I wear to conform not to Your will but to the wills of others. Thank You for sending Jesus to die for the imperfect person behind the mask so that I might die to the expectations of others and be my redeemed self.

---

4   Ryan Neal, "Sleeping At Last," Sleeping At Last, 2016, http://sleepingatlast.com.

5   Kim Eddy, *Enneagram for Beginners: A Christian Guide to Understanding Your Type for a God-Centered Life* (New York, NY: Penguin Random House LLC, 2020), 53.

Day 16 Reflections:

How has your ability to adapt in different friendships allowed you to make a positive impact?

What mask are you currently wearing to gain a sense of approval or belonging?

When has a fear of rejection led to a fear of intimacy? What is one step you can take to be more authentic with someone?

→ Respond

Create two columns on this page or in a journal. In one column, write down how you see yourself. In another column, write down how you think others see you. Under your list, write down one action step you can take to reveal your authentic self more to others and to merge those columns together.

People Pleasing

For am I now seeking the approval of man, or of God? Or am I trying to please man? If I were still trying to please man, I would not be a servant of Christ.

—Galatians 1:10

WE "HEART TYPES" (TWOS, THREES, AND FOURS) have been compared to a peacock. We don't shy away from opportunities to show off our impressive, glorious feathers.[1] For unhealthy heart types, it's as though every act—no matter how apparently selfless—comes with a plea, "Please see my beautiful feathers; validate me, see me!" All of the prominent Enneagram authors teach that Twos do this by *seducing*—a superpower of powerful attraction (sexual or otherwise)—that can be used for good or bad. In fact, Twos are often misinterpreted by others as flirtatious when in fact they are just operating out of their social

> Flattery and insults raise the same question: What do you want?
>
> –Mason Cooley

---

1   Richard Rohr and Andreas Ebert, *The Enneagram: A Christian Perspective* (New York, NY: The Crossroad Publishing Company, 2001), 88.

style of being affectionate and outgoing. The Two proverb is "you can catch more flies with honey than with vinegar."[2]

Unhealthy Twos may use their power of seduction to gain the favor of important people, get what they want without having to ask, or "buy" ongoing acceptance and appreciation through lavishing praise on others. One of the Two's greatest gifts is affirmation: "Praise flows from [Twos'] lips as honey from a bee's comb."[3] But when Twos overuse this gift it can deteriorate into flattery, offering excessive or insincere praise to get approval.

Because Twos often don't realize how much they lavish their affection on others, others in the room might get jealous or feel devalued if they aren't on the receiving end. Along those same lines, a Two can overdo their affection to the point others feel "engulfed" by their love—rushing toward others with *too much* praise, generosity, or messages, convincing themselves, "I can make anyone like me" whether it's the pastor or local barista. Twos tend to believe there are only two kinds of people in the world: "those who like them, and those who don't know them well enough yet to know they like them."[4]

> Pleasing others eventually leads to our own massive displeasure.

If you feel slightly convicted at this point, don't worry. I'm with you! Honestly, before doing my research, as a Three with some heavy Two overlap, I used to think that you could never give *too much* encouragement. That sounds crazy to me! But this journey has made me reflect on how much I use excessive affirmation (often unintentionally) to gain the admiration of important people or to lay the groundwork for a friendship that says, "If I make you feel good, then you'll never make me feel bad."

On the positive side, healthy Twos have full permission to use their contagious sweetness for good. You show us how to be sentimental and wear our hearts on our sleeves. When we go through seasons of discouragement that feel like

---

2   Chestnut, *The Complete Enneagram.*

3   Wagner, *Nine Lenses on the World*, 216.

4   Chestnut, *The 9 Types of Leadership*, 83.

poor-tasting medicine, you are the proverbial "spoonful of sugar that helps the medicine go down."[5] You are also very good at building people up with sincere encouragement, acknowledging and calling out our unique talents and gifts, and often the first to say "I'm sorry" in conflict because you want to quickly reconcile your beloved relationships.

The Good News for Helpers is that your desire to draw others in is a reflection of the *image Dei*. Jesus said, "And I, when I am lifted up from the earth, will draw all people to myself."[6] The Greek word for *draw* (ἐλκύω) means to pull others in with an attractional power.[7] When you use your personality to draw others to Jesus, you mirror the work of the Holy Spirit whose mission is to bear witness about Him.[8] In short, God wants to leverage your ability to win others over as a central force for drawing others into the life-giving resurrection life of Jesus!

Ask yourself today, "Am I now seeking the approval of man, or of God?" For Paul concludes, "If I were still trying to please man, I would not be a servant of Christ."[9] Paul says you can't be a people-pleaser and a God-pleaser at the same time. You have to choose today which one you will be. Remember, serving God also serves you well. Pleasing others eventually leads to our own massive displeasure. If you don't want to allow others the power to give or take away your worth, then rest in God's approval, which prevails over all other opinions.

→ Pray

Father, thank You for creating me uniquely to draw others to Jesus. Forgive me for sometimes giving others too much power to speak over the worth You've already given me. I acknowledge that my happiness doesn't depend on pleasing others. By the Spirit's power, help me to exchange flattery for honesty and leverage my gifts to call others' attention to You.

---

5   Moser, *The Enneagram of Discernment*, 235.

6   John 12:32

7   Strong's greek: 1670. ἐλκύω (helkó) — to draw, accessed September 28, 2022, https://biblehub.com/greek/1670.htm.

8   John 15:26

9   Galatians 1:10

Day 17 Reflections:

What have you been able to accomplish for God using your magnetic personality?

Why is it so important to you to be liked? How do you feel when you are unable to please someone?

How do you flatter others in an attempt to make them like you (praise, gifts, favors, etc.)? Do you use powerful charisma or more of a subtle sweetness and charm? Explain.

How would resting in God's approval create a healthier you and transform your relationships?

→ Respond

Give someone honest feedback without sugarcoating it. Remember, if you share what you believe to be right, their reaction doesn't automatically make you wrong or get to be a measure of your worth.

Day 18:

Crazy Generous

> *By this we know love, that he laid down his life for us, and we ought to lay down our lives for the brothers. But if anyone has the world's goods and sees his brother in need, yet closes his heart against him, how does God's love abide in him? Little children, let us not love in word or talk but in deed and in truth.*
>
> —1 John 3:16-18

WHEN I FIRST MET SCOTT, I WASN'T expecting such a warm greeting. Though he is a megachurch pastor with a lot on his plate, he made me feel like his best friend from our first conversation. My church was starting a new bilingual community in our city, so we contacted Scott for financial support. Before even beginning the conversation of financial support, he insisted on treating our pastoral staff to lunch, wanting to become friends before we became partners. Soon after, Scott ended up giving us much more than we asked for to help fund our new church plant. Then, as if that wasn't generous enough, he invited

> We make a living by what we get, but we make a life by what we give.
>
> –Winston Churchill[1]

---

1   Richard B. Gunderman, *We Make a Life by What We Give* (Bloomington, IN: Indiana University Press, 2009), 56.

us on stage on Sunday morning to recruit their entire church to be part of our launch team. In case you are wondering, this kind of crazy generosity is rare in a day when churches can be territorial and protective of their tithers.

Scott's generosity of spirit—made tangible by his material generosity—is a beautiful example of a healthy Two seeing a "brother in need,"[2] not loving in word only but also in deed. Twos are gratified when they give something of value to others that helps them grow.[3] It may be their time, attention, money, or other valuable resources. They have a unique combination of both emotional and physical support. Twos are always looking out for the welfare of others even when it's inconvenient. My father (the epitome of a Helper) comes over to watch our son—who's on the autism spectrum—washes our windows, mows our lawn, touches up the paint, and then asks for any other work we might need him to do!

One of the best places we see this theme of crazy generosity is the story of Ruth and Boaz.[4] During the time of the judges, a famine swept the land of Israel. Out of options, Elimelech decided to move his wife and two sons from their ancestral home to the land of their pagan enemies: Moab. There, the boys grew into men and married local Moabite women. But Elimilech died and was soon followed by both of his sons, leaving Naomi alone in a foreign land with her two Moabite daughters-in-law, Ruth and Orpah, as her only companions. Around this time, the famine in Judah ended and Naomi longed to return home to her native soil. Her daughters-in-law—now also bereft of support—begged to come along, but she instructed them to return to Moab to find new husbands, have children, and start again. Orpah agreed with this sensible command, but Ruth clung to Noami and replied, "Where you go I will go, and where you stay I will stay. Your people will be my people and your God my God."[5]

> Twos are gratified when they give something of value to others that helps them grow.

---

2   1 John 3:17

3   Don Riso and Russ Hudson, *Personality Types: Using the Enneagram for Self-Discovery* (HMH Books, 1996), 70-71.

4   Pearl Gervais, Diane Tolomeo, Remi J. De Roo, *Biblical Characters and the Enneagram: Images of Transformation* (Victoria, B.C.: Newport Bay Publishing, 2002), 84-95.

5   Ruth 1:16 NIV

Upon their return, Boaz, a wealthy landowner and relative of Elimelech, allowed and even encouraged Ruth to glean food from his field. This unselfish and generous man rescued Ruth and Naomi out of poverty. Overjoyed with Boaz's generosity, Ruth said, "I have found favor in your eyes, my lord, for you have comforted me and spoken kindly to your servant, though I am not one of your servants."[6] What happened next is completely unexpected: like a healthy Two, Boaz went beyond the kindness of offering Ruth and Naomi a source of food and gifts and offered what no other man was willing to give: *himself*. He stepped into the role of kinsman-redeemer, a Jewish tradition in which a male relative accepts the responsibility to care for—in this case, marry—family in need or danger. Boaz married Ruth, offering her emotional, financial, and physical safety and security for the rest of her life.

The Good News for Helpers is found in Boaz and Ruth's lineage. After they married, Obed was born, who became the father of Jesse, the father of King David, who became a direct ancestor of Jesus Christ.[7] Following the example of His ancestor, Jesus became our Kinsman-Redeemer. He showed compassion for our vulnerable state and grafted us into His forever family. No longer do you have to live off of scraps or live with a fear of being harmed; you've been covered by the providence and protection of Jesus. He doesn't just offer you gifts—He offers you Himself. From now on, remember that Jesus makes you His priority every day, not because you are useful, but because you are *His*.

→ Pray

Jesus, thank You for being my Kinsman-Redeemer. Though I was a stranger, You brought me in, fed me, clothed me, and offered protection. Most of all, thank You for giving the gift of Yourself. I never have to worry about being on my own again. Show me how to use the spirit of generosity You've given me to inspire others to be crazy generous.

---

6   Ruth 2:13

7   Matthew 1:1-6

Day 18 Reflections:

When was the last time you gave something of value to help others grow?

How does the generosity of Boaz inspire you to keep being crazy generous? Who might you be able to show generosity toward today?

How can you go beyond individual generosity toward creating a culture of generosity where you live and work?

→ Respond

Challenge your family or team to do a random act of kindness this week. Afterward, come together to share the impact your generosity made on others.

Your Deadly Sin

Peter said to him, "You shall never wash my feet." Jesus answered

him, "If I do not wash you, you have no share with me."

—John 13:8

OUT OF ALL THE DEADLY SINS POSSIBLE for the Helper, I initially found it a little surprising that *pride* was assigned to Twos. Every person and type struggles with pride, but for the Twos the struggle is less obvious (and therefore more spiritually deadly). When we think of pride, we typically think of more overtly haughty people: conceited, arrogant, or obnoxious know-it-alls and egotists. But there's a form of pride that is even more deadly—the sort that sounds like "I will make myself so indispensable to your life (or team) that you won't be able to get along without me."

> False humility is the pride of not being proud.
> —Michael Bassey Johnson

The lie Twos are particularly prone to believe is: "I am indispensable." Whereas Fives desire to "be like God" in becoming omniscient (all-knowing) and Eights as omnipotent (all-powerful), Twos want to be omnibenevolent (all-loving). They want to become indispensable to others by being *seen* as all-good, all-kind, and all-generous.

When Twos become aware of this secret form of pride in their lives for the very first time it can be painful, but it can also be transformational. For instance, Richard Rohr recalls "what happened to a [Two] … when her mask fell and it suddenly became clear to her what kind of game she had been playing her whole life. She came three days in a row to her office hour with me, and could do nothing but cry uncontrollably. It was a real conversion. She wept over her pride and over the fact that she had always thought she was the most lovable person in the world."[1]

The vice of pride expresses itself in a Two's life when the way they love others becomes "the law" people must abide by. Pride also manifests when Twos believe they are superhuman, taking on more than they can actually handle to make more people happy. Finally, pride rears its ugly head when Twos feel superior for not having any conscious needs themselves while at the same time feeling needed by everyone else.[2]

> Being a disciple of Jesus means allowing others to serve you.

However, the Two's great virtue, humility, counteracts this sin when you begin to let go of your unreasonable expectations of others, limit how much you help others, and get comfortable with "looking needy"—being someone who isn't afraid to ask or receive help. After Peter refused to let Jesus serve him saying, "You shall never wash my feet," Jesus followed up by explaining, "Unless I wash you, you have no part with me."[3] In other words, being a disciple of Jesus means allowing others to serve you too.

In 2 Kings 5, the powerful commander of Syria's army, Naaman, suffered from the terrible disease of leprosy. He was encouraged to travel all the way to Israel to seek healing from the prophet Elisha. Yet when Naaman—the commander of the army that conquered Israel—arrived at Elisha's door, the prophet didn't come out but sent a messenger to tell Naaman to wash in the Jordan River seven times. Naaman refused saying, "Are not Abana and Pharpar, the rivers of Damascus, better than all the waters of Israel? Could I not wash in them and be clean?' So he

---

1 Rohr and Ebert, *The Enneagram*, 124.

2 Chestnut, *The Complete Enneagram*.

3 John 13:8

turned and went away in a rage."[4] But his servants urged him to obey the strange command. Eventually, Naaman set aside his pride, washed in the Jordan seven times, and was miraculously healed![5]

The Good News for Helpers is God is willing to help if you aren't too humiliated to ask or receive it. In fact, when we "boast all the more gladly of my weaknesses" Christ's power comes and rests on us.[6] In Mark 10, a blind beggar named Bartimaeus, shouted, "Jesus, Son of David, have mercy on me!"[7] Though he was scolded by many for being so unashamed with his request, he began shouting even louder! Jesus then called for him, and asked, "What do you want me to do for you?"[8] Bartimaeus gave Jesus a direct request and was healed on the spot. Think about how much Bartimaeus's life changed that day because he wasn't too proud to look needy or helpless. This is actually how God prefers we come to him. As the old "Rock of Ages" hymn goes:

"Nothing in my hand I bring,

Simply to Thy cross I cling;

Naked, come to Thee for dress;

Helpless, look to Thee for grace."

→ Pray

Father, I praise You for being "so full of unfailing love for all who ask for your help."[9] Remind me today that You don't need me but love me still. Help me by Your Spirit to walk in humility, admitting my neediness and limitations, taking a step back to receive Your renewing grace.

---

4   2 Kings 5:12

5   2 Kings 5:14

6   2 Corinthians 12:9

7   Mark 10:47

8   Mark 10:51

9   Psalm 86:5 NLT

Day 19 Reflections:

Which character, Naaman or Bartimaeus, do you identify with more and why?

In what way do you need to cultivate humility: lowering your expectations of others, limiting how much you help others, or getting more comfortable with looking needy?

If Jesus asked you today, how would you answer His question, "What do you want me to do for you?"?

> ### → Respond
>
> Try to catch yourself today telling someone "I don't need anything." Instead be honest about where you feel helpless.

Day 20:

Self-Care

But he would withdraw to desolate places and pray.

—Luke 5:16

IMAGE WALKING INTO YOUR FAVORITE LOCAL SANDWICH shop and coming to the realization that it's a one-woman operation. She's the owner, cashier, sandwich maker, and janitor all in one. Though she's always making sandwiches for her growing number of customers, she never seems to eat. As months of lunch breaks go by, you notice she's beginning to look unhealthy. Once energetic, she now looks pale and exhausted. Though the shop has an abundance of food, she is forgetting to feed herself.[1]

> Sometimes you don't realize you're actually drowning when you're trying to be everyone else's anchor.
>
> —Anonymous

Does this story sound familiar? Helpers have a way of satisfying others while starving themselves. That's why Suzanne Stabile advises Twos to not only make sure everyone has a seat

---

1 Illustration adapted from Tim Ellmore, "The Starving Baker for Teachers," Growing Leaders, September 9, 2011, https://growingleaders.com/blog/the-starving-baker-for-teachers/.

at the table but to take their seat as well.[2] As we mentioned yesterday, it's easy for Twos to forget their limitations, imagining themselves as "a spring bubbling up from within instead of an empty pond needing rain from without."[3] It's also easy for Twos to believe the lie that others' needs are more important than my own. Therefore, the growth path for all Twos will be to become more selfish (in the best sense of the word). It will feel very uncomfortable at first, but it's necessary if you want to be full enough to pour into others' lives.

Spiritual growth looks like no longer holding guilt for taking care of yourself first and ignoring that little voice inside your head that says, "Why are you being so selfish!" Rather, it's making a commitment to nurture your own growth and development, coming up with your own support plan before making one for others, offering yourself the same level of care you give to others. As Jerome Wagner puts it, "Do unto yourself what you have been doing unto others."[4]

In her book *Take Care of Your Type*, Christina Wilcox shares a wonderful plea: "Helpers, you're allowed to be the shoulder to cry on, while also crying on someone else's. You're allowed to give, and you're allowed to take. You're allowed to give advice, and you're allowed to receive it. You don't have to be everything to everyone—because you're worth so much more than that. You have your own heart, soul, mind, and desires that deserve to be supported and cheered for by others! It doesn't make you selfish, it makes you human."[5]

> Jesus couldn't live without solitude and neither can you.

Enneagram theory says that Twos move to type Four in health. When this happens, Twos become more comfortable with being alone, sitting in silent introspection; they begin to express their needs and feelings, and often take up creative pursuits. For some, this looks like singing, painting, writing poetry, or photography—anything that allows you to do something for yourself for a change. It is choosing to ignore the call of duty at times and instead learning to play and do something that brings you joy and pleasure even if it feels selfish.

---

2 Stabile, *The Path Between Us*, 87.

3 Wagner, *Nine Lenses on the World*, 221.

4 Ibid., 222.

5 Wilcox, *Take Care of Your Type*, 31.

Carve out a few hours every week on the calendar to turn off your phone and just do whatever you want to do!

We learn from the Gospel of Luke that Jesus often withdrew from people to practice solitude. At the start of His ministry, Jesus spends forty days fasting in the wilderness to prepare for His mission—forty days without doing anything for anyone! Before Jesus chose the twelve disciples, He went off alone to pray, then throughout His ministry, He often sneaked off to a solitary place to pray. Finally, at the end of His life, He sought peace and hope in the garden of Gethsemane. Jesus couldn't live without solitude and neither can you.

The Good News for Helpers is that opportunities for "small solitudes" abound, such as the early morning moments in bed, drinking a cup of coffee, or sitting in traffic. Furthermore, you can designate your own quiet place—a special corner of a room, special chair, or find a park, church, or retreat center—whatever helps you become quiet and centered to hear the whispered words of God. Here is the most important thing to remember: Self-care without soul-care is self-ish care. True, holistic self-care includes resting from activity and saturating our souls in the One who makes us whole.

→ Pray

Father, You are a fountain of living water, and I am not. If Jesus depended on solitude for rest and guidance, how much more must I depend on it? Forgive me for ignoring my hunger pains and resisting your invitation to feed my hungry soul. Free me from the guilt of having to tell others no so that I can say yes to my own wellbeing.

Day 20 Reflections:

When do you feel guilty for taking time for yourself?

What things in life bring you the most joy?

How does your schedule need to change for you to prioritize self-care?

➜ Respond

Slow down to do something life-giving today for your pure enjoyment rather than for someone else.

Finding Your Strength

Be strong and courageous. Do not fear or be in dread of them, for it is the

Lord your God who goes with you. He will not leave you or forsake you."

—Deuteronomy 31:6

DID YOU KNOW THAT BEING *NICE* IS not God's highest value for you? Being pleasant and agreeable are great qualities, but they will only get you so far in relationships, work, and personal development. Being the nicest guy or gal in the room may lead you to feel humble, but it will also lead to feelings of weakness and disempowerment. You may resist speaking up in relationships, never saying what you truly think or forfeiting your ideas or preferences to keep others happy.

> Take care to get what you like, or you will be forced to like what you get.
>
> —George Bernard Shaw[1]

As my Two friend once admitted, "I typically let go of what I want and need to keep the peace, even though I have no peace at all. But I've learned that peace isn't real if it's not working for both people."

When feeling powerless, Twos may "hulk out" and explode, unable to control their emotions.

---

1 Henry Cloud, *9 Things You Simply Must Do to Succeed in Love and Life: A Psychologist Learns from His Patients What Really Works and What Doesn't* (Nashville, TN: Thomas Nelson, 2004), 9.

Or they may withdraw passive-aggressively, assuring us that "Nothing is wrong!" when their sulking communicates that *everything* is wrong. When unhealthy, Twos may take on the role of martyr (similar to an unhealthy Four) in a last-ditch effort to get their needs met. As Riso and Hudson explain, "Their real (as well as their exaggerated) suffering allows them to feel like martyrs who are overburdened by their sacrifices for others, although they may well overrate their efforts on others' behalf. Healthy Twos do not talk much about their own problems; lower-average-to-unhealthy Twos talk about little else. Past operations, scars, traumatic experiences, and health scares of all sorts are paraded before others in an attempt to elicit signs of concern and love."[2]

The solution to avoiding a martyr-syndrome and experiencing more agency is to regain your sense of power. When Twos move to the high side of type Eight, they find their God-given power and free themselves of the need for others' approval and appreciation.

> The more you pay attention to yourself, the more others will pay attention to you.

They become assertive, authentic, and autonomous. One such biblical leader is Deborah—the famous Old Testament judge, prophetess, and self-titled "mother in Israel."[3] In Judges 4, she summoned Barak, the commander of Israel's army, and asked him why he hadn't gone into battle after the Lord commanded him to do so. One can hardly blame Barak: their enemy, King Jaban, had oppressed Israel for twenty years and had nine-hundred chariots that could slice through foot soldiers like butter. Undaunted by the enemy or her general, Deborah publicly called out Barak, lighting a fire under him to obey the Lord's clear command.

We need more Deborahs in the church today to hold leaders accountable! Rather than piling on from the sidelines or simply taking over, Deborah gave Barak the opportunity to fulfill his obligation to protect Israel, but the commander had a condition: "If you will go with me, I will go, but if you will not go with me, I will not go."[4] Barak found Deborah to be a source of spiritual strength and so she

---

2   Riso and Hudson, *The Wisdom of the Enneagram*, 142.

3   Judges 5:7

4   Judges 4:8

agreed, advancing with the army to see the Lord deliver their oppressive enemy into their hands. Later, they even sat down together for a songwriting session![5]

Deborah is an incredible role model for all Twos—a brave warrior and caring mother whose presence others depended on for strength. As the only female judge in the Old Testament, Deborah wasn't just a quiet supporter but an up-front leader. Seeing conflict as a good thing, she lovingly confronted Barak, refusing to sugarcoat the truth. Unlike many Twos, she didn't buy into the lie that says "I can get what I want if I please people the right way." Rather, she stood up for herself and God's people by making a clear declaration.

The Good News for Helpers is that you were not created to be a "yes-man or yes-woman" but were made in the image of the God who boldly and courageously makes declarations.[6] Throughout the Scriptures, God makes His heart known. It is precisely because God has disclosed Himself so clearly through Christ that we can have intimacy with Him and flourish under His wisdom. As an image-bearer, you must pursue courageous transparency over insecure obscurity by declaring your convictions, speaking up for yourself, disagreeing with others, and saying no more. The more you pay attention to yourself, the more others will pay attention to you.

→ Pray

Father, out of Your mouth come mighty declarations. Help me make known my thoughts and feelings as You do. Forgive me for deferring the authority You've given me to others to make decisions I'm capable of making. Grow my self-confidence so I can use the power You've given me to serve the people around me like Deborah did.

---

5   Judges 5

6   Isaiah 46:9-11

Day 21 Reflections:

When have you let go of your desires and needs to keep the peace or others happy?

What about Deborah's story motivates you today? When was the last time you made yourself clear or confronted someone like Deborah? How did it feel?

God does not withhold His true colors from you. How does that truth bless you today?

> ### → Respond
>
> Use an "I" statement with a firm voice, upright posture, looking directly at the person, believing your needs are just as important as theirs. Try to not worry about their response. Instead, express yourself—and leave the results to God.

Day 22:

Stress Triggers

*And Moses lifted up his hand and struck the rock with his staff twice, and
water came out abundantly, and the congregation drank, and their livestock.
And the LORD said to Moses and Aaron, "Because you did not believe in
me, to uphold me as holy in the eyes of the people of Israel, therefore you
shall not bring this assembly into the land that I have given them."*

—Numbers 20:11-12

STRESS IS A NATURAL FACTOR OF LIFE, so our goal as people seeking to live healthily and consciously is not to avoid all stress but to be aware of and respond to it in positive ways. When we are unaware of our stress triggers—for instance, some of the most common for Helpers are to feel unheard, unneeded, taken for granted, or un- and underappreciated—we may find ourselves "suddenly" at the breaking point, ready to blow up in spectacularly public ways.[2]

> No pressure, no diamonds.
>
> –Thomas Carlyle[1]

---

1 Iam A. Freeman, *Seeds of Revolution: A Collection of Axioms, Passages and Proverbs, Volume 1* (Bloomington, IN: iUniverse,World Harvest, 2014), 74.

2 Beth McCord and Jeff McCord, *Becoming Us: Using the Enneagram to Create a Thriving Gospel-Centered Marriage* (Nashville, TN: Morgan James Publishing, 2020).

Other Type Two stressors include receiving negative feedback or rejection or failing to receive proper recognition for your work. For instance, does it really bother you when people don't say "thank you" after you've gone the extra mile for them? Jesus knows what that's like. On the way to Jerusalem, passing between Samaria and Galilee, He entered a village and was met by ten lepers, all crying out for healing. After making them clean and sending them away to meet with the priest (the only one who could affirm the miracle and allow them to reenter society), only *one* returned and fell on his face at Jesus' feet, giving thanks.[3] Though saddened by the lack of gratitude, Jesus remained calm. The same cannot always be said for a Two who feels slighted.

Sometimes, the anger or stress has an obvious outside source; all too often, though, a Two's stress is self-induced. You may overextend yourself, committing to too many charities, volunteering too many hours, or listening way longer than necessary to other's problems. Later, you will privately kick yourself for doing too much: *Why do I promise them that? Why did I sign up for that? Why did I give so much of my time?* Nevertheless, when the time rolls around to follow through, there you are.

> God loves and helps the ungrateful along with those who return on bended knees.

Under these conditions, Twos may appear outwardly positive, but rest assured: the anger and stress are slowly building within. Some of the warning signs that you are turning into a walking steam kettle are that you work even harder, blame others, become demanding or manipulative, act out inappropriately, or experience physical symptoms in your body.[4]

When positive and encouraging Twos move to the unhealthy side of Eights under stress, others will quickly find "that beneath the velvet glove is an iron fist."[5] The Bible presents many case studies of people who lashed out publicly because of stress. One of those most infamous and visible meltdowns (one that

---

3   Luke 17:11-19

4   Riso and Hudson, *The Wisdom of the Enneagram*, 143.

5   Sandra Maitri, *The Spiritual Dimension of the Enneagram: Nine Faces of the Soul* (New York, NY: Jeremy P. Tarcher/Putnam, a member of Penguin Putnam Inc., 2001), 121.

came with steep consequences) is Moses. More than once, he seemed to throw up his hands, telling God he would rather die than deal with the unfaithful Israelites another moment. While the meltdowns often occurred in private, Moses's public tantrums took place before the entire nation—like the one at Meribah, when he struck the rock.[6]

The Good News for Helpers is that there is a way to bend without breaking. You are loved by a God who is "merciful and gracious, slow to anger and abounding in steadfast love and faithfulness."[7] He is long-suffering toward us, meaning He is willing to wait with patience long before showing anger, and because He has a long fuse, God does not react, retaliate, or punish quickly but is merciful and forbearing. And just as Jesus received the world's hostility on the cross yet reverberated love in a remarkable demonstration of self-control, you too can pour out grace on even the most ungrateful and lazy people you know. God is willing to give you a longer fuse so you can act honorably before all and "uphold [God] as holy in the eyes of the people"[8]—the very thing Moses failed to do at Meribah.

The next time you feel the kettle getting hot, ask clarifying questions rather than assuming others are being purposefully selfish or ignoring you. If someone was in the wrong, seek to forgive quickly and release any resentment. Finally and most importantly, cling to the truth that Christ loves and wants you and that you no longer need to depend on others' approval, gratitude, and encouragement.[9] Remember, they may not acknowledge or reciprocate your help, but God does, and He loves and helps the ungrateful along with those who return on bended knees.

---

6   Numbers 20:10-13

7   Psalm 86:15

8   Numbers 20:12

9   McCord and McCord, *Becoming Us.*

→ Pray

Father, thank You for sending Your Son to be our example of someone who bent without breaking. Through temptation, opposition, persecution, and even death, He did not fold. Oh Lord, let the same compassion flow out of me that flowed out of Jesus when He was struck on the cross.

Day 22 Reflections:

What triggers your stress most often? What past stressful experience might actually be considered trauma?

Describe a time when you could have lashed out at someone who deserved it but instead were slow to anger, merciful, and gracious.

What steps can you take now to prevent a public meltdown like the one Moses experienced?

→ Respond

Because others may be able to see the warning signs before you do, ask someone to share how they can tell when you are stressed out.

Hulking Out

What causes quarrels and what causes fights among you? Is

it not this, that your passions are at war within you?

—James 4:1

SOME OF MY MOST EMBARRASSING MOMENTS HAVE come from allowing stress, frustration, or annoyance to build up suddenly, leading me to lash out--most often at family members. For instance, when my two boys won't stop fighting, I can turn into the Hulk without notice: "*Stop, stop, stop, STOP!*" After multiple attempts to calmly get those rowdy, name-calling boys under control, I flip out. I go from calm to crazy in no time flat.

> Expectations are resentments waiting to happen.
>
> –Anne Lamott[1]

Yesterday, we looked at Moses' public meltdown, striking the rock at Meribah and embarrassing himself in the process. It's a crucial story for Helpers because Moses, who "hulked out" before an entire nation, is also known for being "more humble than anyone

---

1   Brené Brown, *Rising Strong: How the Ability to Reset Transforms the Way We Live, Love, Parent, and Lead* (New York, NY: Penguin Random House, 2017), 140.

else on the face of the earth."[2] His big reaction is unexpected because we (and the people of Israel) have grown accustomed to a long-suffering Moses––a man who is neither childish and angry nor destructive; he's quite the opposite.

The mishap at Meribah is a reminder that even the most loving people "hulk out" sometimes. This is the move Twos make when their "old self"—that unhealthy side of Type Eights they try so hard to keep buried within—comes out. Though it will be painful, becoming more aware of this move will save you over and over again, helping you prevent burnouts, breakups, or blowups. The most common reasons for Twos hulking out are sensing a lack of appreciation or care (toward you or a group of people you care about), feeling taken for granted, or feeling controlled by others' needs. When unhealthy Twos can no longer repress their feelings, they may punish (or fantasize about punishing) others, manipulate people into feeling guilty for underappreciating them, boast about how much more they've done, or make threats to exert control. As Claudio Naranjo says, Twos have the capacity to "make love and war."[3]

> When you feel your anger toward others increase, look within first.

The deceptive thing about this move is that the anger always feels justified. Twos know it's never okay to have an image that's openly aggressive. Instead, they convince themselves their venting is virtuous, righteously calling out those who are, to them, acting so obviously from selfish motivations. While there certainly *are* selfish monsters out there that need to be called out, sometimes a Two's target is simply someone who hasn't given them what they want.

When you feel your anger toward others increase, look within first to discern if it's really your own expectations that are the issue. As the apostle James asks, "What causes quarrels and what causes fights among you? Is it not this, that your passions are at war within you?"[4] Taking James' advice, ask yourself, *Am I angry because they are not repaying my help the way I want? Am I bitter because it feels*

---

2   Numbers 12:3 NIV

3   Claudio Naranjo, *Character and Neurosis: An Integrative View* (Nevada City, CA: Gateways/IDHHB, 1994), 171.

4   James 4:1

like they no longer need me the way I want to be needed? If so, God invites you today to "receive others as they are, rather than as you want them to be."[5]

The Good News for Helpers is that God forgives you for not fulfilling His perfect expectations. The cross has cleared all records of wrongs, including the times you lacked appreciation toward God or took Him for granted. When unhealthy Twos forget the gospel, they will lack grace toward others, becoming stenographers in the courtroom of life, recording everything, ready to pull out others' records of wrongs and recite them verbatim in a moment's notice. But keeping score never leads to fulfilling relationships. Rather, a follower of Jesus is one who leads with forgiveness, saying, "Father, forgive them, for they know not what [I want]."[6]

To keep that childish or angry "old self" from rearing its ugly head, keep *forgiving* as you have been forgiven and work more on *declaring* your needs. For example, saying, "I wish I didn't have to clean the house," is not the same thing as, "Would you clean the house this time?" I know you might be thinking, "I shouldn't have to tell them," but remember, others aren't wired with your strengths and need a little extra nudge to act sometimes. Give them the benefit of the doubt. Know that most people genuinely care and will show up if you ask.

→ Pray

Father, remind me today that Your Son Jesus came to help but was unsupported and taken for granted. As it is written, "Foxes have holes, and birds of the air have nests, but the Son of Man has nowhere to lay his head."[7] Help me forgive others as much as You have forgiven me and express my hurts before I hurt others.

---

5   Calhoun and Loughrige, *Spiritual Rhythms*, 83.

6   Luke 23:34

7   Luke 9:58

Day 23 Reflections:

When was the last time you hulked out at someone? What was the unmet need or expectation behind the anger?

Who do you need to forgive for not appreciating you enough or taking you for granted? Is there anyone you need to ask forgiveness from? Explain.

How can you make your needs crystal clear right now to a family member, friend, or boss?

→ Respond

Don't beat yourself up when you catch yourself moving toward others too aggressively. Congratulate yourself for noticing, take a deep breath, and clearly communicate what you need.[8]

---

8   Cron and Stabile, *The Road Back to You*, 128.

Reciprocal Relationships

Now Laban had two daughters. The name of the older was Leah, and the name of the younger was Rachel. Leah's eyes were weak, but Rachel was beautiful in form and appearance. Jacob loved Rachel. And he said, "I will serve you seven years for your younger daughter Rachel."

—Genesis 29:16-18

THE FIRST EPISODE OF ANCIENT ISRAEL'S VERSION of *The Bachelor* covered the Bible's first love triangle: Jacob, Rachel, and Leah. Jacob, the runaway trickster, fell madly in love with his uncle Laban's younger daughter Rachel and offered to work for him for seven years to marry her. Though Laban agreed to the union, Jacob was so consumed with working for Rachel that he completely missed what was happening around him—including any cues that perhaps his uncle wasn't totally on-board with giving his younger daughter in marriage before the older, Leah, had been properly tended to. So, on Jacob and

> There comes a time when you have to stop crossing oceans for people who wouldn't even jump puddles for you.
>
> —Anonymous

Rachel's wedding night, Laban pulled a fast one on his famously shifty son-in-law, and Jacob slept with Leah.

With the new marriage now consummated, Leah may have found the weight of insecurity lifted off of her after years of comparing herself to her apparently more attractive sister. That is, until Jacob realized he slept with the wrong girl and angrily agreed to tend his uncle's flocks for another seven years for Rachel. After all the tears and agony Leah most likely experienced from Jacob's rejection, you would think she would redirect her love elsewhere; instead, she went on to bear many children for Jacob, thinking to herself every time, "*now* my husband will love me."[1]

This pursuit--romantic or otherwise--of people who aren't able or willing to recognize their worth is an unhealthy habit for Twos. Insecure or immature Helpers are some of the most likely people to find themselves in unbalanced relationships. At first, the "opposites attract" rule has them pursuing a partner who is shy, socially awkward, or has difficulty with the banal work of making a life together. This will initially make the Two feel like they have much to offer, which brings a type of security to the relationship for them.[2] Similarly, in their professional lives, they may work "with very young children, old people, orphans, drug addicts, alcoholics, or terminally ill patients, all of whom need their services but who are unable to adequately return the Two's love and attention."[3]

> You must love yourself enough to let go of the Jacobs in your life.

Pursuing such people is noble, needed, and a great blessing to the world. However, the problem comes when Twos inevitably receive little to no mature responses from these individuals. Or, if their love is reciprocated, they are never truly sure if others love them for who they are or what they do. I'm sure it's severely painful for you to come to the realization that the other person in your relationship isn't concerned with spending as much time or energy on you as you do for them.

---

1   Genesis 29:31-34

2   Melanie Bell, Kacie Berghoef, *The Modern Enneagram: Discover Who You Are and Who You Can Be* (Berkeley, CA: Althea Press, 2017), 107.

3   Riso and Hudson, *The Wisdom of the Enneagram*, 140.

What's the solution? Well, if you haven't already, Riso and Hudson advise, "Learn to avoid falling in love with fixer-uppers."[4] In other words, pursue relationships with those who can fully reciprocate your love and are not in need of "rescuing." Find people who love spending quality time with you—people who don't need anything other than to simply enjoy being around you. To accomplish this, you will first need to stop seeing yourself as not being worthy of others' love and help. You will also need to humbly accept the natural flow of giving and receiving. This means you must enter relationships with people who want to do the work of exchanging that give-and-take dynamic love as found and displayed in the Trinity.

The Good News for Helpers is that God sees those who feel invisible in their relationships. Though Leah was constantly overlooked by Jacob, God saw her and blessed her with children, an ancient sign of divine favor. You, too, are seen and matter deeply to God. Don't give in to the temptation to think you are unworthy of love. Cultivating the Two's prime virtue of humility includes seeing yourself as God sees you—worthy of life-giving friends and partners. It also means you must love yourself enough to let go of the Jacobs in your life. After Leah conceived another child and bore Jacob their son, Judah, instead of saying, "now my husband will love me," she said, "This time I will praise the Lord."[5] When Leah stopped giving her sons to Jacob to get love and instead received her sons as a gift from the Lord, she found true freedom.

→ Pray

Father, Your love is truly reciprocal. As John said, "this is love, not that we have loved God but that he loved us."[6] Give me the wisdom to know which earthly relationships I need to let go of, even if I feel I can offer them so much value. Help me open my hands and receive more life-giving relationships that will help me to live a more fulfilling life.

---

4   Ibid., 141.

5   Genesis 29:35

6   1 John 4:10

Day 24 Reflections:

Who have you tried to help/rescue but received little in return? What lessons did you learn?

____

____

____

Do you typically make the first move to call, visit, encourage, apologize, or forgive? What can you do to make your relationships more reciprocal?

____

____

____

What relationships would you put in the "beneficial," "permissible but not beneficial," and "not beneficial" categories?

____

____

____

→ Respond

Take a week off from reaching out to people. Helpers typically reach out first and others get used to this dynamic. As a self-care exercise, let others reach out to you first this week.[7]

---

7   Wilcox, *Take Care of Your Type*, 35.

Necessary Endings

I am the true vine, and my Father is the vinedresser. Every branch

in me that does not bear fruit he takes away, and every branch

that does bear fruit he prunes, that it may bear more fruit.

—John 15:1-2

WE TOOK A CLOSE LOOK AT THE love triangle of Jacob, Rachel, and Leah yesterday. Unfortunately, the drama continued even after Leah gave up on trying to earn Jacob's love through childbearing. Rachel, beloved of her husband but bereft of children, became consumed with jealousy and followed the matriarch Sarah's example, handing over her maidservant to sleep with Jacob as a last-ditch effort to provide him with children. Not to be outdone, Leah lowered herself to Rachel's level and decided to play this game as well, handing over her maidservant.

This childbearing competition continued for a while, and years and children later, we can

> Every new beginning comes from some other beginning's end.
>
> —Seneca, Roman philosopher[1]

---

1 Peter Scazzero, The Emotionally Healthy Leader: How Transforming Your Inner Life Will Deeply Transform Your Church, Team, and the World (Grand Rapids, MI: Zondervan, 2015), 280.

see a great mountain of bitterness was raised between the sisters. In one telling episode, Rachel asked her sister for some of her son's mandrake roots (which were seen as an aphrodisiac and infertility aid) and Leah, who had now gone some time without bearing Jacob a child--likely due to his preference for Rachel--snapped, "Is it a small matter that you have taken away my husband? Would you take away my son's mandrakes also?"[2]

As I see all of this drama unfolding, I really wish that Leah would have just walked out on Jacob back when he first rejected her, yet in that ancient time and place, she didn't have the freedom to make such a decision. But *you do*. I know ending a friendship or relationship might feel as painful as pulling a tooth without an anesthetic, but eventually, you have to decide if the pain of keeping things the same is greater than the pain of making a change.

The biblical language for this process is called *pruning*. The world is a garden, Jesus is the Vine, and the Father is the Vinedresser. The Father not only cuts off the fruitless branches but prunes the fruitful ones. Pruning is not comfortable, but it is a necessary process that involves cutting sick, dead, or overgrown branches. As it is with the physical world, so it is with your soul: you must pay attention to how your relationships are affecting your life. Perhaps you simply have too many overgrown branches you are trying to take care of. Remember, every yes you say to one branch requires a no in another.[3] Maybe you need to acknowledge that some of your branches are sick and need to be cut off for you to become healthy.

Why is it so hard for us to let some relationships go so that new branches can grow? Helpers may idealize those they merge with or live with a false sense of hope: "If I wait it out, things will get better, or they will change." But we cannot live forever believing people will change if they show no desire or action toward that end--what you need is concrete hope. If the objective data doesn't lead you to conclude that things will change six months or one year from now, it must be pruned—it has to go. These things must have their necessary ending, or you will come to the end of yourself.

---

2   Genesis 30:15

3   Stabile, *The Path Between Us*, 91.

The Good News for Helpers is that you don't have to feel bad about pruning because it's a natural part of life. Are you carrying any guilt or shame over past relationships you've had to end? You don't have to any longer. King Solomon said there is "a time to keep and a time to cast away."[4] You have God's permission to prune. Don't automatically assume the problems in your relationships are your fault. Don't assume things will automatically get better. Don't assume you can keep the relationship going by covering the commitments for the both of you.

Don't be afraid to make a change. We often miss the invitation to open the door to new beginnings because we haven't embraced the truth of necessary endings: as author Peter Scazzero reminds us, "Death is a necessary prelude to resurrection."[5] It was through Jesus' death that our new life began. Likewise, some things must die so we can truly live. It will be hard to let go, and you will grieve, but joy always comes in the morning.[6]

→ Pray

Father, You are the Vinedresser who will complete the good work You started in me. You say a true disciple will bear fruit. Help me live more frutifully by taking action to prune my life and relationships. Give me the faith to believe resurrection life will come out of necessary endings.

---

4   Ecclesiastes 3:6b

5   Scazzero, *The Emotionally Healthy Leader*, 274.

6   Psalm 30:5

Day 25 Reflections:

What guilt or shame have you been carrying over past relationships that you need to let go of?

In what ways have you found it difficult to let people go? How have you tried to hold on to people?

Where have you been living with a false hope that things will change? What boundaries need to be set? How much time will you give before a necessary ending is required?

> **➜ Respond**
>
> Write out briefly what you want to be true of your relationships five years from now versus what they will actually look like if you don't let go of the things you know you need to leave behind.

Thriving at Work

Then I said to them, "You see the trouble we are in, how Jerusalem

lies in ruins with its gates burned. Come, let us build the wall

of Jerusalem, that we may no longer suffer derision."

—Nehemiah 2:17

NEHEMIAH, THE FIFTH CENTURY BC LEADER WHO supervised the rebuilding of Jerusalem was a God-follower who exemplified faith in action. After hearing Jerusalem's walls were broken down and its gates destroyed by fire, he wept for days—praying and fasting. Then, rather than waiting in helpless grief for God to send someone else, Nehemiah realized he was the answer to his own prayer. He traveled to Jerusalem, secretly surveyed the rubble, and determined the size and scope of the project before committing to

> You will not have a meaningful life without work, but you cannot say that your work is the meaning of your life.
>
> —Timothy Keller[1]

---

1   Timothy Keller and Katherine Leary Alsdorf, *Every Good Endeavor: Connecting Your Work to God's Work* (New York, NY: Penguin Books, an imprint of Penguin Random House, 2016), 27..

it. Then, to everyone's surprise, this cupbearer got permission to rebuild from the king of their captors, Emperor Artaxerxes.[2]

Similarly, Helpers have the same incredible work ethic displayed by Nehemiah. Twos have a "doing" orientation, displaying selfless service as they energetically support others and lift the mood of their team. They bring the fun, host great parties, and orchestrate positive experiences and meaningful connections, which strengthen relationships in their teams, organizations, and communities. They excel at being at the right place at the right time for people, able to truly "rejoice with those who rejoice; mourn with those who mourn."[3] If businesses or organizations don't recruit Twos, they will be at a deficit when it comes to taking good care of the needs of their customers and employees.[4] The preeminent people-persons, Twos also tend to have a knack for outreach and promotion, bringing in more people to their cause or organization.

People love working with Healthy Twos, seeing them as workplace treasures who represent them well, support them behind the scenes, and become indispensable allies. Their superpower is building community by connecting and supporting people. Their highly developed interpersonal skills thrive in positions where there is lots of people contact[5] as they help the organization go further faster by cultivating relationships and empowering people through positivity and encouragement. Their primary focus of attention, which can also be a derailer, revolves around the "people" aspect of work—the needs and feelings of others. That's why Twos often find themselves in helping professions such as counseling, Human Resources, teaching, office administration, or health care. More extroverted Twos may find themselves in the spotlight as actresses, actors, or motivational speakers.

> Remind your team that people are the mission.

To thrive in the workplace, Beatrice Chestnut advises Helpers to remember strong emotions are still frowned upon in many workplaces and, while times

---

2 Nehemiah 1:3–2:8

3 Romans 12:15 NIV

4 Chestnut, *The 9 Types of Leadership*, 86-87.

5 Cron and Stabile, *The Road Back to You*, 123.

are changing, it's good to be aware of your emotional triggers so that you can learn how to express your feelings in a way that will be well-received by others. You also need to recognize that your scorecard for success is vastly different from others. While a successful day for you includes meaningful connections with others, for many of your coworkers it is productivity, achieving goals, or helping the company with the bottom line. Knowing that your co-workers prioritize different things will help you not to view them as insensitive, but just different.[6] Rather than judge, leverage your gifts to remind your team that *people* are the mission.

The Good News for Helpers is though your labor in the home or workplace can be toilsome and frustrating, you'll be able to look back like Nehemiah and say, "for the good hand of my God was upon me."[7] The work Nehemiah set out to do appeared outrageous and was threatened at every step by corruption and intimidating neighbors. And yet, God used Nehemiah to do more than his helpless people could ask or imagine during a time of despairing captivity.

Working in the king's court, Nehemiah could have settled for playing a supportive role but instead chose to step into the lead role and inspire others with a grand vision. Nehemiah is a role model for Twos who often prefer to be the power-behind-the-throne, leading indirectly so that they don't have to deal with face-to-face hostility or rejection. Twos are sometimes hesitant to be thrust into the leadership spotlight because that would mean a bigger target on their backs, but remember, just because you are supportive doesn't mean God always wants you to take on a supportive role. Be courageous and lean confidently into your relational and practical gifts to lead your people to accomplish more than you or anyone else thinks is possible.

---

6 Chestnut, *The 9 Types of Leadership*, 93.

7 Nehemiah 2:8

→ Pray

Father, forgive me for often settling for a support role when Your desire is for me to lead with courage. Help me pray bigger, bolder prayers as I dream about how to repair the broken walls and gates in my city. Because You've given me incredible determination and practical gifts, use me today to inspire and align others to Your grand plan.

Day 26 Reflections:

When have you used your gifts to build a flourishing community by connecting and supporting people?

How can you change your schedule or job description to thrive more at work? Are you doing what you want or what someone else wants?

What seemingly impossible project would you like to accomplish or role would you like to step into if you knew God's hand was on you?

→ Respond

Plan a party, retreat, or bonding activity that will facilitate positive experiences and meaningful connections to strengthen the relationships on your team or in your group.

Blind Spots at Work

For you have died, and your life is hidden with Christ in God. When Christ

who is your life appears, then you also will appear with him in glory.

—Colossians 3:3-4

TWOS CAN REALLY STRUGGLE WHEN THEIR WORKPLACE culture doesn't value people to the same level they do or is led by someone who comes off as cold or unavailable. Helpers put people first--period. Their passion is to develop successful *people* more than processes and procedures. Ultimately, no matter the exact nature of the work, their vision is to create a well-knit, flourishing community walking the same path together.

> When you are immune to the opinions and actions of others, you won't be the victim of needless suffering.
>
> —Miguel Ruiz[1]

As we discussed yesterday, Twos bring many strengths to the workplace, yet like the rest of us, they can struggle when their strengths are overdone: in this case their people strengths. Before they notice, encouragement

---

1   Don Miguel Ruiz, *The Four Agreements: A Practical Guide to Personal Freedom* (San Rafael, CA: Amber-Allen Publishing, 1997).

can deteriorate into insincere flattery, unsolicited help into intrusiveness, and sensitivity into living off other people's struggles and drama. This is why it's so important to be aware of your blind spots and learn strategies for counteracting them. After all, your workplace does not need your help so much as it needs you to be healthy.

Perhaps the biggest area that will hold you back in the workplace is needing people to like you: Twos are highly responsive to approval but crushed by disapproval. This need for approval affects every work dynamic and relationship, but let's first zoom in on your relationship to authority. Twos often have an internal conflict between ambition and wanting to please their leaders, looking to them to fill their deep need for validation and recognition. Twos always ask themselves, "How can I get them to endorse my project?" Twos can experience tremendous hurt if their work goes unnoticed or unrecognized. If there is no positive feedback or affirmation coming their way, they can feel anxious because they don't know where they stand in the organization.

While people pleasing can lead to dependence on receiving the acceptance of those above you in the organizational chart, it may also lead you to sugar-coat the truth with your colleagues and anyone for whom you are responsible, making it difficult to provide honest, candid feedback. You may avoid conflict altogether or become a feedback fugitive when all constructive criticism feels like rejection.

> Your workplace does not need your help so much as it needs you to be healthy.

Because Twos like being around those who truly appreciate them, they may also have a blind spot of "playing favorites." For this type, favoritism at work often takes the shape of thoughts like, *People who really appreciate what I do for them are more important than others and deserve a larger share of my attention.*[2] Finally, because Twos focus so much on others, they can easily get wrapped up in others' business and forget about their own work priorities.

Beatrice Chestnut offers some helpful advice to overcome these and other blind spots: Try taking on less responsibility for others' happiness and focus more for

---

2   Mario Sikora, Maria Jose Munita, *The Enneagram Guidebook: An Introduction to Personalities@work* (N.p., 2020), 29.

your own needs and feelings. Ask for permission first before you help someone to ensure you aren't being intrusive, and notice when you are trying too hard to get someone to like you through excessive compliments, gifts, or acts of service. Accept your emotional intuition as a strength but also learn to process your own emotions, dial them back when needed, or express them in more conscious ways. Lastly, work on developing a sense of self-worth from the inside out so that outside validation and approval adds to your self-worth, rather than shaping it. If your identity is based on a shifting thing like accolades, recognition, or likability, you'll soon find your self-worth swept away with what remains of your approval.[3]

The Good News for Helpers is when we trust in Christ, building our lives upon His solidity and finding our identity securely hidden within Him, He becomes both our solid rock and tower of refuge––the strong tower that holds our fragile sense of worth in safe keeping. What is needed to counter negative self-esteem isn't a bigger ego, but rather a more accurate view of yourself hidden in the love of Christ. In Him, you can overcome the lie that says you are only as good as your last praise or as bad as your last criticism. In Him, it's possible to have a thick skin and retain a soft heart—to be sensitive to others' feelings while also allowing them to be merely the weather surrounding the mountain of our identity in Christ.

→ Pray

Father, I have found myself searching for self-worth in acknowledgment from others. Forgive me for all the ways I have tried to build my reputation on the sands of changing outward approval. Thank You for sending Your Son to go to the cross. Without any protection, He received the criticism for sin that I deserved so that He might be my rock of protection.

---

3 Chestnut, *The 9 Types of Leadership*, 103.

Day 27 Reflections:

How do your personal values conflict with the Western workplace?

How has needing people to like you affected your work relationships and projects?

What is one piece of advice you'd like to work on from today's reading?

> **➜ Respond**
>
> Instead of waiting for a future opportunity such as an exit interview to express your dissatisfaction, be bold today and ask for a change you would like to see happen in your workplace.

World-Class Hospitality

Do not neglect to show hospitality to strangers, for thereby

some have entertained angels unawares.

—Hebrews 13:2

AT THE TENDER AGE OF EIGHTEEN, AGNES joined a teaching order of nuns called the English Ladies. From there she was eventually sent to teach geography at a high school in Calcutta, India. But young Agnes found herself drawn to the rundown slum neighborhood behind the school and, after becoming director of the school, Agnes began taking students into the slum to take care of the sick. After a while, she became dissatisfied with the limited amount of work she could do on these short visits, so in 1946, she declared, "I have to leave the convent and help the poor by living among them."[2] Today, thousands of workers have followed in this courageous and compassionate

> The hunger for love is much more difficult to remove than the hunger for bread.
>
> —Mother Teresa[1]

---

1   "Mother Teresa's Most Inspiring Quotes," CNN (Cable News Network, September 1, 2016), https://www.cnn.com/2016/08/30/asia/gallery/mother-teresa-inspiring-quotes/index.html.

2   Christian Feldmann, *Träume beginnen zu leben: Grosse Christen unseres Jahrhunderts* (Freiburg, Basel, Vienna: Herder, 1983), 76.

woman's footsteps, taking vows of chastity, poverty, and obedience to give free service to the poorest of the poor.[3]

Agnes, who we now know as Mother Teresa, presented all of the mature qualities of a Two though, due largely to her strength and dogged pursuit of justice, many are convinced she was an Eight. Either way, Mother Teresa didn't try to proselytize people with words alone but displayed with her daily actions that "The only thing that really converts is love."[4] She fought for the "widows and orphans" of our day—the most unsupported, neglected group of people on the planet—setting up hospices on the street saying, "They have lived like animals. They should at least die like human beings."[5] Just as we saw Deborah challenge Barak on Day 21, Mother Teresa challenged the prime minister Lothar Späth of Baden-Württemberg, Germany in 1982 to allow refugees to seek asylum in Germany: "Open your doors and God will bless you."[6]

"Don't count the cost" is the motto Mother Teresa kept reminding her fellow co-workers in the gospel. Like a mature Two, she sacrificed her own comfort and livelihood to show world-class hospitality, restoring dignity to countless people and expecting nothing in return. Rightfully so, she was eventually acknowledged on the world stage for her tremendous work, receiving the 1979 Nobel Peace Prize. In her acceptance speech she said, "I am very happy to receive [the prize] in the name of the hungry, of the naked, of the homeless, of the crippled, of the blind, of the leprous, of all those people who feel unwanted, unloved, uncared, thrown away of the society, people who have become a burden to the society, and are ashamed by everybody."[7]

> Healthy Twos serve out of conviction, not compulsion.

Helpers and hospitality are synonymous. Without fail, you are loving, warm, kind and "are like a home in human form—a place of safety for those in need of

---

3   Rohr and Ebert, *The Enneagram*, 131.

4   Ibid., 132.

5   Feldmann, *Träume beginnen zu leben*, 86.

6   Ibid., 88.

7   "The Nobel Peace Prize 1979," NobelPrize.org, accessed September 28, 2022, https://www.nobelprize.org/prizes/peace/1979/teresa/acceptance-speech/.

rest."[8] You open up the doors to your heart and home, welcoming all to come in and experience their belovedness. You understand that hospitality is qualitatively different from entertaining—guests are not there to impose but to become members of your very own family. You make your guests want to curl up on your couch and never leave![9]

AJ Sherrill says hospitality is a discipline that comes natural to all Twos and is one they must steward responsibly: "This can take the form of hosting dinners for guests, serving on mission trips, contributing to local projects, serving in the local church or an organization, or simply being available to others in a time of need. Creating a monthly dinner for friends, acquaintances, or strangers is a helpful rhythm and discipline, especially in a harried and individualistic Western context."[10] The only caveat is that Twos should practice hospitality without expecting anyone to return the favor: as Sherrill reminds us, Healthy Twos serve out of conviction, not compulsion.[11]

The Good News for Helpers is found in the command "welcome one another as Christ has welcomed you."[12] Christ welcomed you into the fold when you were poor and needy, not because He had to, but because He wanted to. As someone who has tasted the hospitality of God, go and leverage your gift even more, remembering you will be entertaining angels along the way.[13] When you show off that world-class hospitality like Mother Teresa did, it's a reminder to us all that Jesus said the greatest in the kingdom will not be those who like to recline at the table but those who serve.[14]

---

8   Case, *The Honest Enneagram*, 60-61.

9   Calhoun and Loughrige, *Spiritual Rhythms*, 89-90.

10   Sherrill, *The Enneagram for Spiritual Formation*, 69-70.

11   Ibid.

12   Romans 15:7

13   Hebrews 13:2

14   Luke 22:27

> **→ Pray**
>
> Father, I praise You for welcoming me in and treating me as family. Thank You for entrusting me with the incredible gift of hospitality. Use me as part of Your redemptive plan to restore dignity and worth to the least of these where I live and work. Guide me to whatever bold step You want me to take next to bring Your loving care to a world in desperate need.

Day 28 Reflections:

What inspires or compels you about Mother Teresa's story?

How have you used your gift of hospitality recently? How would you like to use that gift again soon?

Where can you implement an ongoing rhythm of hospitality in your home, church, or workplace?

> **→ Respond**
>
> Invite someone beyond your friendship circle to dinner at your place this week.

Finding Yourself

" 'And you shall love the Lord your God with all your heart and with all your soul and with all your mind and with all your strength.' The second is this: 'You shall love your neighbor as yourself.' There is no other commandment greater than these."

—Mark 12:30-31

The most painful thing is losing yourself in the process of loving someone too much, and forgetting that you are special too.

–Ernest Hemingway[1]

WHEN YOU WALK INTO SOMEONE'S HOME AND notice a portrait hanging on the wall, your eyes are most likely drawn to the image rather than the frame. A good frame supports and enhances what lies within rather than drawing attention to its own grandeur. Helpers are like that frame, and those they love are like the portraits in the middle. Without realizing it, they forget to look at themselves, as their attention continually focuses on the people in the frame with whom they have merged.

---

1   Vancil, *Self to Lose Self to Find*, 72.

One Helper describes their experience: "When I go on a silent retreat, I literally can't think about anything but my relationships with my husband, my kids, my friends, and my colleagues. When I pray, I pray for other people. When I read, I think about how what I've read will be helpful to someone else. With such a focus on others, there is little energy left for knowing ourselves … ."[2]

Being a people person is great, but it could lead you to erase yourself entirely if you don't slow down and pay attention to yourself; self-care is step one of caring for others. A religious leader asked Jesus what the greatest commandment was, and He replied, "Love the Lord your God with all your heart," but He continued, saying "The second is this: 'You shall love your neighbor as yourself.'"[3] Though enough of us have difficulty as it is with the "loving others" part, what strikes me is the phrase "as yourself." Jesus assumes we are loving and taking care of ourselves first, but for many of us that is simply not true. If He were speaking to Twos specifically He might say, "You shall love yourself as much as you love others."

Loving yourself means growing in autonomy and independence by discovering your own identity. The trap Twos fall into is telling themselves "I can make people like me by being less like me" which leads you to disown the parts of yourself that make you truly valuable. As Beatrice Chestnut explains, "In this way they get caught up in a vicious cycle of shape-shifting to attract others, then needing more support and validation from the outside to support a weakened sense of self. It's only by taking the risk to find out who they are—and letting go of the need to make everyone like them—that they find their way out of the trap."[4]

> You shall love yourself as much as you love others.

As the saying goes, "Humility is not thinking less of yourself, it's thinking of yourself less."[5] True humility is seeing yourself as God sees you, neither discounting yourself nor giving away too much power in exchange for a trinket of approval. So, when others see you, do they see the *real* you or just the "supportive"

---

2 Stabile, *The Path Between Us*, 80.

3 Mark 12:30-31

4 Chestnut, *The Complete Enneagram*.

5 Rick Warren, *The Purpose Driven Life: What on Earth Am I Here For?* (Grand Rapids, MI: Zondervan, 2012).

image you struggle to project?—because there's a big difference between the two. Though your superpower is showing up for others, the next growth step is learning how to show up for yourself and to put on display a portrait of the real you for the world to see.

Like a healthy Four, get some alone time this week to be introspective and do a deep dive of your likes, dislikes, and interests, listing out the things that are really important to you. What do you get fired up about? What tugs at your heartstrings? Make sure to get out and try new things too, pushing yourself toward new experiences that may draw out surprising parts of you. If you have a better sense of these things, you can move from supporting people in positions of power to owning your own power and defining your agenda instead of letting others do that for you.

The Good News for Helpers is that you don't have to apologize for "I am" statements because you are a reflection of the great "I AM," with whom "there is no variation or shadow due to change."[6] Now you can ask the question, "Who am I?" rather than "Who do they want me to be?" The good news is that merging with Jesus—losing yourself in Him—actually leads to finding and becoming more of who you were meant to be.

→ Pray

Father, give me the independence I need to prevent me from losing myself in others. When my mind wanders toward thinking of others too much, bring my attention back to myself. Help me create healthy separation from others so I can fully see my divine design and purpose. Give me the gift of seeing myself through Your eyes rather than the eyes of others.

---

6   James 1:17

Day 29 Reflections:

When was the last time you lost yourself and merged with someone else? What led you to disown valuable parts of yourself or give away too much power?

Why is it so difficult to love yourself as much as you love others? What do you need to change to make this a reality?

If you were to paint an authentic portrait of the real you, what would you want others to see? What makes you unique from everyone else?

➜ Respond

Because Twos find themselves when they are alone, put a day of solitude on the calendar to explore your dreams, desires, interests, and goals to find out who you are apart from others.

Day 30:

Comforted to Comfort

Blessed be the God and Father of our Lord Jesus Christ, the Father of

mercies and God of all comfort, who comforts us in all our affliction,

so that we may be able to comfort those who are in any affliction,

with the comfort with which we ourselves are comforted by God.

—2 Corinthians 1:3–4

"JESUS WEPT."[2] THOSE WORDS REPEATED THROUGH MY lowered head as I sat at my desk, my own tears welling up. A long road of infertility had rocked my marriage, leaving dreams crushed and hopes deferred. For years, my wife cried and cried, unable to believe we'd ever see a miracle, and to this day, still no miracle. I, on the other hand, didn't cry but instead kept telling her to "have faith."

Looking back, I can see that what I had was not faith but naivety and that telling anyone

> God does not comfort us to make us comfortable, but to make us comforters.
>
> –John Henry Jowett[1]

---

1   Warren W. Wiersbe, *With the Word: The Chapter-by-Chapter Bible Handbook* (Nashville, TN: Thomas Nelson, 1993), 65.

2   John 11:35

who is struggling to simply "have faith" is never a good call--faith is neither the opposite of tears nor a cure-all for our struggles and doubts. I now understand I was suppressing my emotions by naively assuming everything would work out, but this was just an unconscious strategy to hide from my own doubts and pain. In so doing, I suppressed Lindsey's struggle, dodged her emotions, failed to offer God's presence, and held fast to stoicism when I should have been sowing tears.

Thankfully, we joined a small group of believers who felt stuck in various ways. During one of our sessions, the leader pointed his finger at me and sternly said, "David was a man who grieved and was called a man after God's own heart. You haven't done that." Those stern words shocked me out of passivity, and the next morning, as I sat reading the story of Lazarus, I finally broke open. Coming across the powerfully short line, "Jesus wept," I heard God tell me: "Lindsey's tears are *My* tears." And for the first time since we began our struggle, I too wept.

In the years that followed, God provided us with two miracles, Zane and Zeke, by way of infant adoption. But our life didn't get any easier. Our youngest, Ezekiel, was diagnosed with autism spectrum disorder around the age of four. After he was kicked out of multiple schools, Lindsey chose to homeschool him. When all of the typical parenting strategies don't work, it's easy to feel like a failure. But God has graciously sent us many fierce empathizers such as Chase, who I mentioned in Day 2. She has written us countless encouraging words over the years like this one:

> You are an enormous source of comfort to us in our times of trouble.

> God called you to an especially hard task, but you've done it for seven years without ever once cursing your son or speaking a bad word about him to others. The thousands of hours you have spent in your home over the years—that no one else will ever see or know about—Jesus sees that. It may be no consolation to you, Lindsey, but a woman who has reworked her entire life to tirelessly sacrifice for her child, day in and day out, is the exact opposite of a failure. You have never given up. You have always kept choosing love even on your darkest days. Even if it doesn't feel like you'll ever be appreciated for it, Zeke is held secure in one fact

alone—mom and dad will always come back for me. Zeke sees Jesus in you because you radiate Him. You are no failure. You are an inspiration.

On another occasion, after one of my Sunday sermons, Chase walked up to the front row where Lindsey and I were sitting. She was only able to let a few words escape before she laid her head on my wife's shoulder and began weeping. To this day, when anger and frustration begin stirring inside of me on the really hard days, I often think back to this precious, tender moment in the middle of a packed sanctuary and remember that Chase's tears are God's tears.

The Good News for Helpers is that God "comforts us in all our affliction, so that we may be able to comfort those who are in any affliction."[3] Be prepared today, because God regularly calls upon Twos to be His go-to agents of comfort. Twos are the most empathetic of all personality types, and with this power comes great responsibility. You have the superpower of being able to put yourself in others' shoes and feel what they feel, almost as if these were your own feelings—whether it's a stranger suffering on television or a long-time friend sitting right next to you. Know that you are an enormous source of comfort to us in our times of trouble when you display your fierce love, weeping with us in an embrace of loving understanding.

➜ Pray

Father, my soul is comforted as I see Your Son, Jesus, weeping at Lazarus' funeral. As I find my way through a stoic society, remind me that tears are Your gift to me so that I can feel what You feel. Do not let me waste my tears, but sow my tears into this dry land filled with other hurting people who need to be nourished with empathy.

---

3   2 Corinthians 1:4

Day 30 Reflections:

How does knowing Jesus weeps on your shoulder bring you comfort today?

When was the last time God used you to comfort someone through your words or actions? How can you make this a regular rhythm in your life?

What has been the biggest trial of your life? How does your past suffering show you who God might be sending you to comfort next?

→ Respond

Talk to someone in your church this week about starting a care ministry or getting involved with an existing one.

Trusting God with Your Family

[God] said, "Take your son, your only son Isaac, whom you love,

and go to the land of Moriah, and offer him there as a burnt

offering on one of the mountains of which I shall tell you."

—Genesis 22:2

THERE AREN'T MANY PASSAGES IN THE BIBLE that make Lindsey cringe as much as that one. What would you say if God asked you to give up one of your closest family members? Well, in one of Scripture's foundational narratives, God asked Abraham to do just that: to take his only son, the son of promise, and offer him as a sacrifice. Though this story sounds barbaric to our modern ears, it would've been par for the course in this ancient Near Eastern context—just another story of the gods asking for everything from their worshipers. Though as with most difficult stories in the Bible, there's much more going on under the surface.

> Let your children go if you want to keep them.
>
> —Malcom Forbes[1]

For Helpers, family is not an afterthought but a first thought. Twos make incredible parents, caregivers,

---

1 Malcom Forbes, *The Sayings of Chairman Malcom: The Capitalist's Handbook* (New York, NY: Harper & Row, 1978).

mentors, and compassionate leaders. Author Jacqui Pollock teaches that Twos provide love, nurture, and a sense of belonging and safety. Their social skills, friendliness, generosity, and approachability rub off on the whole family. Children of healthy Twos always have their needs met and are blessed to have a parent who always listens without judgment. Best of all, they will grow up receiving an unending stream of encouragement, raising their self-esteem.[2] In short, "Twos are the embodiment of the good parent that everyone wishes they had."[3]

On the other hand, as with anything in our lives, family can become an idol that we cling to for dear life instead of living open-handedly like Abraham. Pollock explains that unhealthy Twos fear no longer feeling wanted or needed if they don't have a role to play. That's why this type so easily becomes the proverbial "helicopter parent," constantly hovering and smothering their children under overprotective arms. Twos can't bear to see their loved ones suffer even one ounce of pain, so they often resort to doing everything for them rather than letting the necessary skills for life develop on their own. Other side effects of being overly involved might be family members feeling controlled, which could lead to long-term resentment. Lastly, when you start feeling depleted emotionally and physically, and vastly unappreciated, you may be tempted to project guilt onto others for not acknowledging all you do.[4]

> For Helpers, family is not an afterthought but a first thought.

On the bright side, when Twos are healthy, they will loosen their grip on their loved ones. They will encourage independence, allowing others to learn some things the hard way. They will offer support without rescuing. Being aware of the temptation to please, healthy Two parents will guard against being overly permissive and work on saying no more, becoming okay with some confrontation, realizing that good character is forged by healthy boundaries and discipline, as well as the organic give and take between parents and their children

---

2   Tracy Tresidder, Margaret Loftus, and Jacqui Pollock, *Knowing Me, Knowing Them: Understand Your Parenting Personality by Discovering the Enneagram* (Carlton North, Victoria, Australia: Monterey Press, 2014), 62.

3   Riso and Hudson, *The Wisdom of the Enneagram*, 126.

4   Tressider, Loftus, and Pollock, *Knowing Me, Knowing Them*, 63.

as each discovers where the real boundaries lines lie. Lastly, they will not flatter in order to be liked more but only offer authentic praise.[5]

The Good News for Helpers is God knows what's best for your family. Will you be brave enough to trust and release them into the arms of their loving Creator? Their entire well-being depends on whether or not you release your plans for them into God's hands. Years ago, I led overseas mission trips with college students, and, inevitably, some parents wouldn't allow their young adult children to come with us––they just couldn't let them go into the world's uncertainty. It's true you must protect your loved ones from danger, but when God calls us to obey, we are called to trust as Abraham—no matter how illogical it feels from a human standpoint. Faith puts our need for safety on the altar because safety is not always God's highest priority.

Abraham, with trembling hands, took the knife and stretched out his hands to sacrifice his son Isaac. At the last minute, the Lord stopped him, saying, "Do not lay your hand on the boy or do anything to him, for now I know that you fear God, seeing you have not withheld your son, your only son, from me."[6] Does this sound familiar? Today, we can say we know God loves us because He did not withhold His only Son, the Son of promise. You can trust God with your loved one because God already gave you His.

→ Pray

Father, thank You for giving me such a strong commitment to my family. Help me remember that You know what's best for them. Loosen my grip so I won't get in the way of them being used mightily for Your purposes. I will surrender all of my fears to you today regarding my family.

---

5   Ibid., 68-70.

6   Genesis 22:12

Day 31 Reflections:

How have your strengths of sacrificial love and encouragement positively influenced your family?

In what ways have you seen over-protectiveness or a need to be liked negatively affect your family?

Which family member do you need to let go of in order to fully entrust them to the Lord? Why?

➛ Respond

Create an "I Surrender" list, and name all the fears or anxieties you can think of regarding one of your loved ones: Will they forget about me? Will they return? Will they be safe? Will they make it on their own? Then surrender all those things to God in prayer.

Expressing Yourself

O Lord, you have searched me and known me! You know when I sit down

and when I rise up; you discern my thoughts from afar. You search out

my path and my lying down and are acquainted with all my ways.

—Psalm 139:1-3

FRED MCFEELY ROGERS WAS THE HOST OF the popular preschool television series *Mister Rogers' Neighborhood*, which ran on public television for thirty-three years. This host, producer, and Presbyterian minister had a remarkable way of helping children identify and work through their emotions using song and puppets. Interestingly, he gave himself a daily reminder of his life's purpose by never deviating from weighing exactly 143 pounds because of its symbolic reminder to spread love: "I" (one letter), "love" (four letters), and "you" (three letters). 1-4-3.

> The greatest gift you ever give is your honest self.
>
> —Fred Rogers[1]

---

1   Fred Rogers, *You Are Special: Words of Wisdom for All Ages from a Beloved Neighbor* (New York, NY: Penguin Publishing Group, 1995), 118.

The New York Post claimed, "Mr. Rogers really was the nicest guy ever;"[2] a man who personally responded to the thousands of letters he received from children, praying for each child by name. But few people ever saw him get angry. Noah Harpster, a screenwriter for the movie *A Beautiful Day In The Neighborhood* starring Tom Hanks said, "The two most important people in Fred's life both say that he didn't talk to them, he didn't share the burden that he was taking on all day. Where did that go?"[3]

Similarly, Helpers are the nicest people in the world *and* the ones we hear the least from regarding their burdens. The first reason for this is that they mistake others' feelings for their own, beginning to believe they either are or are not okay based on the person they are with. Authentic feelings get stuffed when they are at odds with someone they love because if you aren't happy, they aren't happy.

The second reason Helpers don't share what's going on inside is because they tend to have shame about their feelings. They believe their secret needs or darker emotions will be unacceptable or abrasive to others—thereby hurting their positive self-image, making others feel uncomfortable in the process, and potentially risking disapproval, disconnection, or rejection. But repressing feelings to "protect" the relationship actually works against you, preventing authentic, intimate connections with others. As a friend looking in, I want to encourage you not to suffer in this way! We are desperate to see the *whole* you.

I know this will be difficult. As one honest Two said, "My toughest challenge is being open and vulnerable with others. I would much rather listen to you and take on your burden than put my own feelings into words."[4] But, if you take bold, courageous steps to express yourself fully you won't have to keep abandoning yourself "in the service of others." You'll discover that it's possible, by God's grace, to *own all of your feelings without fear*. This is where you can take a few cues from

2   Sara Stewart, "Mr. Rogers Really Was the Nicest Guy Ever," New York Post (New York Post, July 25, 2018), https://nypost.com/2018/01/23/mr-rogers-really-was-the-nicest-guy-ever/.

3   Jason Tabrys, "The Final Lesson from 'A Beautiful Day in the Neighborhood' Is One Worth Holding Onto," (UPROXX, February 7, 2020), https://uproxx.com/movies/a-beautiful-day-in-the-neighborhood-lesson/.

4   Alice Fryling, *Mirror for the Soul: A Christian Guide to the Enneagram* (Downers Grove, IL: InterVarsity Press, 2017), 60.

a healthy Four, the personality type that expresses their full range of emotions, and get in touch with the deep desire to be fully known by others just as God has searched us and known us.

The Good News for Helpers is that Jesus was a kaleidoscope of emotions, expressing the entire spectrum of human warmth and love, anger and frustration, grief and loss. He felt deep compassion toward the sick and infirm, anger toward evil and hypocrisy, grief over death and loneliness, and distress over humanity's waywardness. You can express every emotion to Jesus without fear of rejection. Your emotions aren't too much for Him—and in fact, they make you more like Him.

Fred Rogers said that one healthy way to deal with negative feelings is to bang on the low keys of a piano. That is why the final scene of *A Beautiful Day in the Neighborhood* is such a memorable one: Fred sits alone at the piano; the show is over and the studio is empty. He begins to play, then pounds a few times on the low keys in frustration. He pauses for a few seconds, regains his composure, and resumes his peaceful song.

While there is much to admire about Fred's work, the final scene left me wanting more of "low key" Fred. The world is longing to see the minor keys that make up the melody behind your amazing work. Those closest to you want—need—to hear the low notes that are the driving force behind all the good you're doing. Keep banging on those low keys and trust us to sing along.

→ Pray

Father, I'm thankful that You enjoy searching the depths of my heart. You are the One who is most aware of the darkest parts of me, and yet You have lavished Your love on me through Christ. If there is anything grievous within, please show me. If there is anything I'm still hiding behind, please take it away. I want to live fully transparent before You and others.

Day 32 Reflections:

Why do you think Fred Rogers never shared his burdens with the most important people in his life?

Where do you see evidence of repression of emotions in your life? Who do you tend to withhold your feelings to be liked or not be a burden?

Like the psalmists who minister to us wonderfully through their authentic words, how can you make the shift from the role of listener only to lamenter?

➔ Respond

Get out a piece of paper or digital device and do a brain-dump. Write down all your fears, worries, or stressors. You'll notice that using this technique will help you feel less overwhelmed simply by clearing your mind. It will also give you a list of authentic things to share with others.

When Helping Hurts

Then Job answered and said: "I have heard many such things; miserable comforters are you all."

—Job 16:1-2

AFTER JOB LOST EVERYTHING—HIS SHEEP, OXEN, CAMELS, servants, sons and daughters, and even his health—his friends Eliphaz, Bildad, and Zophar, came to rescue him. They started out on the right foot, showing sympathy through weeping aloud, tearing their robes, and sitting with him in silence. But after seven days, they became impatient. Convinced they knew what was wrong, they wrote long-winded opinion pieces, giving Job their "helpful" advice.

Like Job's friends, our well-intentioned "helping" hurts others sometimes. I know this might sound like heresy, but it's possible

> Train yourself toward solidarity and not charity. You are no one's savior. You are a mutual partner in the pursuit of freedom.
>
> —Brittany Packnett[1]

---

1 Brittany Packnett, "How to Spend Your Privilege," The Cut (The Cut, August 1, 2018), https://www.thecut.com/2018/08/nia-wilson-spend-your-privilege.html.

to love someone *too much*. While healthy Twos are the epitome of loving care, unhealthy Twos can struggle with relational boundaries. This can take the form of getting too personal too fast. They may speed up a degree of intimacy that is not expected by the other person. Others may find themselves "in a relationship" with a Two before they even know what happened.

When an unhealthy Two is bent on establishing a closer relationship, they don't take no for an answer. They keep pressing to connect but often in a way that feels smothering, which ironically pushes others away—the thing Twos fear most. Their love can become demanding, sounding something like, "I'll come over this weekend and help clean your house. Then we can go out to dinner and a movie together." Their persistence and insistence can make a person feel awkward or guilty if they say no.

Healthy Twos are some of the best listeners out there, but unhealthy Twos will offer unsolicited advice and opinions: "You should date this person, try this diet, or change your landscaping." However, they usually aren't conscious of the fact they are doing this; rather, they are thinking to themselves, *I'm not being pushy; I'm helpfully responding to an obvious need.* On the surface, the motives seem pure. It doesn't seem prideful or intrusive at all to be concerned. What's the harm in making sure everyone gets what they need and are happy?[2] But again, help that is not asked for may be hurting more than helping.

> Help that is not asked for may be hurting more than helping.

As a pastor who has been involved in ministry for decades, I'm embarrassed to admit some of the ways I've tried to "help" the underprivileged in our city. Looking back, I had a "savior complex," which happens when you (or your church) find a vulnerable group of people you're led to believe can't live without your resources or solutions. But I've had to check my motives: Am I really doing this for them or for *me*? Am I doing this to boost my self-image? Would I still be willing to serve if I couldn't post pictures on social media so that I can protect people rather than use them as a promotional prop?

---

2   Palmer, *The Enneagram in Love and Work*, 76.

Here is a litmus test for discerning our motives: How much am I willing to *receive* from those I want to serve? Am I willing to serve those in the inner-city *and* be willing to befriend, learn from, do business with, or be led by a leader from that community? Am I willing to admit my emotional or spiritual poverty and *receive* from the very people I want to "help?" In other words, is my helping reciprocal or just one-sided? Love seeks equality, not having agency over someone.

The Good News for Helpers is that you are not responsible for fixing others' problems. Jesus repeatedly asked, "What do you want me to do for you?"[3] Likewise, you can have a low-pressure ministry of helping by saying, "Let me know if you need help" or "I'm here if you need me." Remember that other people's problems are just that—their problems. You can still offer your world-class help with your trademark care, but remember that gospel help involves giving others the space to ask. If they say no, trust that "the Helper"[4] will provide for them outside of you.

→ Pray

Father, I so desperately want to make a difference in others' lives and am willing to make a multitude of sacrifices. But I know I've gone too far at times, speaking out of turn and doing things that weren't asked for because I truly believed it would do more good than harm. Remind me today that my job is not to save but to point people to the One who can.

---

3   Matthew 20:32

4   Holy Spirit

Day 33 Reflections:

How does the idea that you can actually love someone too much sit with you today?

What are some ways you can protect yourself from overstepping in the areas of giving advice and helping? Is there anyone you need to have a boundary conversation with?

Have you ever had a savior complex, looking to "fix" or "save" someone from their problems? How can you change your mindset from seeing others, especially those less privileged, as being vital to your spiritual growth?

→ Respond

Read or listen to the book When Helping Hurts by Brian Fikkert and Steve Corbett, which shows how some poverty alleviation efforts in our city and on short-term mission trips have actually (and unintentionally) done more harm than good. The book is full of transferable principles that will have a far-reaching impact in every facet of a Two's life.

The Beloved Disciple

Beloved, let us love one another, for love is from God, and whoever loves has been born of God and knows God. Anyone who does not love does not know God, because God is love. In this the love of God was made manifest among us, that God sent his only Son into the world, so that we might live through him.

—1 John 4:7-9

I SET ASIDE TIME EVERY YEAR TO write my boys a letter on their birthdays, chronicling all of the memories we made that year. I talk about what our friendships looked like and what I specifically loved about them at that age. I can't wait to give these letters to them when they become adults someday so that they never forget: *I am loved.* No matter where they go or what they succeed (or fail) at in

> I am the chosen child of God, precious in God's eyes, called the Beloved from all eternity, and held safe in an everlasting embrace.
>
> –Henri Nouwen[1]

---

1   Henri J. M. Nouwen, *You Are the Beloved: Daily Meditations for Spiritual Living* (New York, NY: Crown Publishing Group, 2017), 15.

life, I want my sons to always be known by my family and friends as "the sons who were loved."

We are always in danger of missing the point of Christianity: you see, it's never been about getting God "right" with our theology or going through the right motions— it's about *love*. The apostle John, who is thought to be a Helper, doesn't want us to miss the point either in his writings. After experiencing the love of Jesus up close and having been invited into Jesus' inner-circle along with Peter and James, John puts an exclamation point on love as the centerpiece of our faith.

John teaches that *God* is *love*––and that we are only able to know and respond to love because He first loved us, which is demonstrated most clearly through the person and work of Jesus. Do you want evidence that you are a true believer, John asks? Then look at how well you love others. That is the deciding factor. On the other hand, when our faith is all "talk," and we neglect our brothers and sisters, we make ourselves out to be liars.[2]

> You are more than your ability to be there for others.

Richard Rohr points out other themes in the writings of John that will resonate with a Two.[3] In John's own Gospel, he recorded this snapshot of himself at the Last Supper: "Lying back on Jesus' chest was one of His disciples, whom Jesus loved."[4] We see here that John found delight in being loved by Jesus and openly showing his feelings toward Him. Surprisingly, John is the only Gospel writer who included one of the most intimate and memorable acts of love performed by Jesus: the washing of the disciples' feet. For John (and Twos), spirituality is experiential, not just intellectual: "That which was from the beginning, which we have heard, which we have seen with our eyes, which we looked upon and have touched with our hands … and testify to it … ."[5]

After many fled the scene at Calvary, John stayed put, grieving with the women. As Jesus looked down and saw John standing next to His mother, He said, "

---

2   1 John 4:7-21

3   Rohr and Ebert, *The Enneagram*, 127-128.

4   John 13:23 NASB

5   1 John 1:1-2

'Woman, behold, your son!' Then He said to the disciple, 'Behold, your mother!' "[6] Before Jesus gave up His spirit, He entrusted His beloved mother into the supportive and caring arms of John.

John had a shadow side like every other Two. One time, after Jesus and His disciples were rejected after going out into the nearby villages, John became indignant--he "hulked out" and asked Jesus, "Lord, do you want us to tell fire to come down from heaven and consume them?"[7] In another scene, like an ambitious Two seeking to be acknowledged by those in positions of power, he asked Jesus if he could sit at either His right or left hand in glory (a bold request that John conveniently seems to have left out of his own Gospel!).[8]

The Good News for Helpers is though John's life was a mixture of success and failure, in the end, he chose to be known as the disciple "whom Jesus loved."[9] John doesn't let us miss the point: "See what kind of love the Father has given to us, that we should be called children of God; and so we are."[10] As a child, you don't have to press Jesus to be pursued, taken care of, or loved. You already are. Remember today that you are "the child whom Jesus loves." He sees you are more than your ability to be there for others. So before doing anything else today, like John at the Last Supper, recline next to Jesus' chest and simply enjoy being His beloved.

➜ Pray

Father, thank You for fully loving and accepting me just as I am. When I catch myself believing the enemy's lies, remind me that I am Your beloved. My worth is not found in how much I can love others but in how much You love me. Give me strength to open my heart wide today to receive an outpouring of love and affection from You.

---

6   John 19:26-27

7   Luke 9:54

8   Mark 10:37

9   John 13:23 NIV

10   1 John 3:1

Day 34 Reflections:

Does your self-worth depend on your ability to be there for others or by being Jesus' beloved? How do you know?

John says that "perfect love casts out fear."[11] What lingering fears of punishment, rejection, or abandonment would you like God to help you overcome?

Though John speaks at length about loving other Christians, he never mentions loving your enemy. Perhaps forgiveness after rejection was a struggle for him. When do you find it hard to forgive others? Who do you find hard to love?

→ Respond

List the lies you are believing about yourself. Try to identify familial, cultural, or other sources behind the lies. Place your hand over the list and ask Jesus to fully and finally remove these lies within. Then rip up the piece of paper and throw it away.

---

11   1 John 4:18

Wrestling with God

I cry aloud to God, aloud to God, and he will hear me. In the day of my trouble I seek the Lord; in the night my hand is stretched out without wearying; my soul refuses to be comforted. When I remember God, I moan; when I meditate, my spirit faints. You hold my eyelids open; I am so troubled that I cannot speak.

—Psalm 77:1-4

FEARING GOD'S DISAPPROVAL, IT HAS TAKEN A lot of time and effort to replace my "well-worded prayers" with raw emotion, and I still get uneasy saying what I *really* feel to God. Just last month, because I've been in a really hard season dealing with all the challenges that come along with being the parent of an autistic son, I sat down and wrote out a list of twenty questions for God such as: *When will this end? How many more meds will we have to try? Will our son have to depend on us forever? Why aren't we seeing any of the promised fruit of the Spirit?*

> Wrestling with God is a sign of intimacy. You can't wrestle with someone you're far away from.
>
> ~Jon Acuff

Much earlier in the journey, I never would have wrestled with God for answers to such questions. I just assumed that no good Christian would *ever* approach God in any way other than polite and courteous. Similarly, Helpers find it a real challenge to show up with honest emotions. These encouraging individuals seek to stay positive and optimistic in conflict with people they want to please, making the other party feel as if the Two is unwilling to address the real issues. While focusing on the positives and zeroing in on good outcomes *is* a strength, it may be irritating to others when it feels as if the Two is sweeping the real problems under the rug. If these avoidance patterns affect Twos' intimacy with human relationships, you can bet they're a factor in their relationship with God.

One of the foundational tales of the Hebrew people is Jacob's wrestling match with God at the Jabbok River. As darkness fell, someone appeared and attacked Jacob as he laid near the water's edge, and there they struggled until the horizon began to brighten. Suddenly, this person touched Jacob's hip socket, and his hip was thrown out of joint. (Personally, I'm glad my wrestling coach didn't go that far!) In a surprising twist, this perpetual runner, the "soft" one who fled from fights, was finally backed into a corner. It was there, when he could neither win nor escape that Jacob grappled with the Divine. God then said, "Let me go" but Jacob replied, "I will not let you go until you bless me."[1] The change of character was achieved, and Jacob was now ready to take the mantle of Patriarch: "Your name shall no longer be called Jacob, but Israel, for you have striven with God and with men, and have prevailed."[2]

From this story, it appears that God delights in people who aren't afraid to strive and struggle—after all, *Israel* means "one who struggles with God." Though such an aggressive stance may feel counterintuitive to what we think God wants from us, Scripture constantly invites us to boldly assert ourselves—to ask, seek, and knock.[3] Just look at David's psalms. A closer inspection reveals a collection of "wrestling" prayers from someone who wasn't reprimanded for his doubts and

---

1   Genesis 32:25-30

2   Genesis 32:28

3   Matthew 7:7-8

questions or his brutal honesty and boldness but rather was called "a man after [God's] own heart."[4]

Do you wrestle with God? Are you clear with Him on your questions and struggles—the parts of yourself and this world--you want to see changed? Do you pour out your desperate needs, doubts, and anger? Do you remind Him of His character and promises and hold onto Him until you get His blessing?

Rest assured God can take our doubts, anger, grief, and disappointment. Practice replacing your well-worded requests with raw emotion. (See Psalm 77) God won't punish you or be disappointed. You have a Father who is more than willing to step into the ring with you; therefore, "let us then with confidence draw near to the throne of grace."[5]

The Good News for Helpers is that God wants to know you even when all you want to do is hide. He knows why you resist being brutally honest and still invites you into the radical authenticity with Him—and with yourself—for which He made you. You can let Him and others in because there's nothing left to fear. He's waiting to bless you today. Don't let God go until you receive His blessing!

→ Pray

Father, I admit that I sometimes hesitate to bring my burdens to others. I've been ignored and rejected too many times. Thank You for giving me the courage to pour out my heart to You with brutal honesty. I know You can take it. I commit myself to strive for Your blessing every day. Give me the courage to set an example of vulnerability for those around me today.

---

4   1 Samuel 13:14

5   Hebrews 4:16

Day 35 Reflections:

What are you afraid to say to God?

What would it look like for you to measure the success of your prayer life by how honest you are rather than how often you pray or how kind you are?

After his wrestling match with God, Jacob—now Israel—walked away with a limp. What lessons have you learned in life that may have left you wounded but more ready to serve?

→ Respond

Lead a devotional on Psalm 77 with your roommates, family, or small group.

Productive Thinking

And it is my prayer that your love may abound more and more, with knowledge and all discernment, so that you may approve what is excellent, and so be pure and blameless for the day of Christ, filled with the fruit of righteousness that comes through Jesus Christ, to the glory and praise of God.

—Philippians 1:9-11

HAVE YOU EVER LOOKED BACK AT SOME of your decisions and wondered, *What was I thinking?* Have you ever shaken your head in disbelief that you dated someone who treated you horribly? Have you ever procrastinated on your goals or dreams because you were convinced a person or organization couldn't make it without you? At the time, you may have been acting on your feelings, not logic.

> We do not need light or easy love. We need the weight and durability of discerning love.
>
> —Marshall Segal[1]

Helpers are as likely as any type to be the most traditionally intelligent people in the

---

1 "Lord, Give Us Discerning Love: A Prayer for Divisive Days," Desiring God, September 15, 2022, https://www.desiringgod.org/articles/lord-give-us-discerning-love.

room. But Twos are more inclined to think with their hearts first—a trait which has both advantages and disadvantages. When your feelings get turned up and empathy kicks in, you may not give your mind enough time to think about the situation from a logical angle.

Unhealthy Twos swing on a pendulum between feeling and doing, bypassing the mind altogether. However, healthy Twos work toward becoming more objective, letting the facts, not just emotions, guide their decisions.[2]

> Twos are more inclined to think with their hearts first.

For example, if someone looks at you a certain way, it doesn't take long for your emotions to start subjectively coloring in all the details: *they must be mad at me, don't care about me, or don't need me.* In these moments, you must remind yourself not to believe such thoughts until there is actual, concrete evidence—so that you don't color outside the lines of reason. Nine out of the ten things you are stressing about right now may not have a good, logical explanation.

Not giving yourself enough space to think before you act may cause you to read the feelings of others and then act on them too quickly without sufficient reflection. While this daily adventure of urgent twists and turns helping others may feel rewarding, this "pinball machine lifestyle" of bouncing from one need to the next or one person to the next will eventually take all your change. Twos can grow and avoid being pulled in so many directions by coming up with a plan or strategy before moving toward others to help.

The apostle Paul told the church at Philippi he was praying that their commendable love would be filled with more *knowledge* and *discernment.* Discernment is the ability to judge our emotions with logic. When your heart leads you to overdo or overgive, discernment is pausing and asking whether or not it is yours to do.[3] Before jumping into another conversation, serving task, or taxing relationship, discernment asks whether or not you need more time for self-care first. Before telling someone yes today, ask whether it aligns with your goals. Add discernment to your love by asking the question "What should I be doing?" *before* you start asking "What can I do for them?"

---

2 Rohr and Ebert, *The Enneagram*, 129.

3 Stabile, *The Path Between Us*, 83.

Toward this end, Drew Moser advises Twos to assemble a personal "advisory board": a few trusted voices around you who can help discern which opportunities, requests, and invitations you have time and energy for.[4] This doesn't mean gathering more "yes friends" who are affirming and always take your side, but those friends who you know will offer constructive criticism and be voices of reason.

The Good News for Helpers is that you have been given the "Spirit of wisdom"[5] who fills you with the mind of Christ.[6] This means you have all you need today to respond to others' needs from a balanced soul, thinking *for* yourself rather than *from* someone else's emotional experience. Because of the Spirit's guidance, you don't have to worry about being led astray by your feelings. In Christ, you have what it takes to think productively so you can be protected from acting irrationally. Today, call upon the Spirit to add knowledge and discernment to your selfless love "so that you may approve what is excellent, and so be pure and blameless for the day of Christ."[7]

→ Pray

Father, I feel pulled in so many directions by people who need me. Give me the same discernment as Jesus, who said no to keep His focus on His purpose, going to Jerusalem to fulfill the greatest act of love the world has ever seen. Give me that same discernment so that I can fulfill all of the good works You've prepared in advance for me.

---

4   Moser, *The Enneagram of Discernment*, 254.

5   Ephesians 1:17

6   1 Corinthians 2:16

7   Philippians 1:10

Day 36 Reflections:

How does "thinking with your heart" have its advantages when it comes to loving God and others?

What important thing should you do but keep putting off for the sake of others?

What can you do to honor your feelings without allowing them to be your guide?

→ Respond

Create a list of the biggest tasks you need to prioritize each week and do these first before chipping in to help others.

The Lord Is My Shepherd

The Lord is my shepherd; I shall not want. He makes me lie down

in green pastures. He leads me beside still waters. He restores my

soul. He leads me in paths of righteousness for his name's sake.

—Psalm 23:1-3

I'M SURE AT ONE TIME OR ANOTHER you were asked during an ice-breaker to choose an animal that best describes your personality. If I had to choose one for you, I would say Helpers remind me of a mama or papa bear—affectionate and lovable—but with a ferocious side when it becomes necessary to protect your loved ones. However, the biblical metaphor most often used for God's people is a lot less impressive—sheep. Sheep are needy, not that smart, difficult to train, prone to wander off and get lost, in danger of being

> The strange thing about sheep is that because of their very make-up, it is almost impossible for them to be made to lie down ...
>
> –Phillip W. Keller[1]

---

1   W. Phillip Keller, *A Shepherd Looks at Psalm 23* (Grand Rapids, MI: Zondervan, 2019), 24.

attacked, easily frightened and confused, and totally dependent on a shepherd to keep them from drowning or falling off cliffs.

Arguably the most popular and quoted Psalm in the Bible is Psalm 23: "The Lord is my Shepherd." David, a shepherd himself, knew each sheep in his flock, fed them, led them, and protected them from predators. When making a case to go after Goliath, he told King Saul that whenever a lion or bear came and took one of his lambs, he struck it down and killed it.[2] Though David was a strong and victorious protector, he chose to humbly put himself in the place of a sheep and magnify the Lord as his Shepherd.

Considering that Twos are always shepherding others but have so many personal needs of their own that go unmet, I think it's significant that in the very first line of this psalm, David said, "I shall not want." Next, he said his Shepherd "makes me lie down in green pastures." Notice the Lord didn't *ask* him to lie down, but *made* him. I laugh, because practically the only way you can get an average Two to lie down is by force.

> Saying no to solitude is not a rejection of others but a rejection of the Lord's invitation to restore your soul.

Why is the Lord's invitation to restful solitude—to come and lie down in green pastures and listen to the calming, burbling streams—so challenging for Twos? One of the reasons is that some Twos say they get anxious when they are alone. As Rohr explains, "When they are alone, the ceiling falls on their head. Meditation and prayer 'in a quiet little room' for long make them anxious because nobody is there to reinforce them and be close to them, and because they are afraid to find nothing in themselves except a black hole or alarming unrest."[3] Mature Twos however are those who have spent significant time alone, learning not only how to relate to others but also to themselves.

---

2   1 Samuel 17:34-36

3   Rohr and Ebert, *The Enneagram*, 116.

When Twos are accustomed to playing the role of giver rather than receiver, choosing solitude may feel like they are rejecting everyone else.[4] But as we see in Psalm 23, saying no to solitude is not a rejection of others but a rejection of the Lord's invitation to restore your soul.

The Good News for Helpers is that the Lord isn't afraid to tell you exactly what you need, making you lay down in green pastures until all of your "wants" are taken care of. As your Shepherd, He knows the sound of your voice, where you like to graze, what "greener" pastures you tend to wander off to, and comes running when He hears your bleating cries. When you walk through the valley of the shadow of death, You are comforted by His strong presence and staff, which He not only uses as a walking stick but as a weapon against your enemies. Because He will never stop knowing, feeding, leading, and protecting you, you can be sure that goodness and mercy will follow you wherever you go.[5]

Your solitude doesn't have to be in a dark prayer closet; it can be walking on your favorite trail trail or simply sitting alone on your porch; you can engage with God in nature or during physical activity if that seems less daunting at first.[6] Here are four questions I reflect on whenever I get away to help you get started during your time of solitude: *Where do I feel burdened? Where do I feel blessed? What do I feel God calling me to do? Where do I need to wait on God?*

→ Pray

Father, I praise You for not only being an authoritative King but a caring Shepherd. Thank You for sending Your Son Jesus to be the "Good Shepherd" who willingly laid down His life for the sheep.[7] Help me not to get so focused on shepherding others that I forget Your invitation to be known, fed, led, and protected. Because I have You, I shall not want.

---

4 Moser, *The Enneagram of Discernment*, 253.

5 Psalm 23:6

6 Moser, *The Enneagram of Discernment*, 253.

7 John 10:11

Day 37 Reflections:

Why do you find it hard to be alone? What fears or obstacles get in the way?

In what ways does a "shepherd" provide a good picture of God? What is it about "sheep" that makes them a good picture of us?

When and where can you go once a month to get solitude?

→ Respond

Plan a day of solitude and answer these questions with the Lord: Where do I feel burdened? Where do I feel blessed? What do I feel God calling me to do? Where do I need to wait on God?

The Heart of the Church

If the whole body were an eye, where would be the sense of hearing? If the whole body were an ear, where would be the sense of smell? But as it is, God arranged the members in the body, each one of them, as he chose. If all were a single member, where would the body be? As it is, there are many parts, yet one body.

—1 Corinthians 12:17-20

Christ prays in me, Christ works in me, Christ thinks in me, Christ looks through my eyes, Christ speaks through my words, Christ works with my hands, Christ walks with my feet, Christ loves with my heart.

—Mother Teresa[1]

WITHOUT HELPERS, THERE WOULD BE NO CHURCH. The best phrase that I can think of for Twos is that they "show up." When my church did a food pantry during the pandemic, our Twos showed up. When many people decided to give up on church after the pandemic, our Twos showed up. When our church hosted a block party for our neighborhood school last month, our Twos showed up.

1   Leonard Allen, *Contemporaries Meet the Classics On Prayer* (West Monroe, LA: Howard Books, 2003), 195.

Helpers appreciate the local church because it gives them a vocabulary for their values and provides them with a place to talk about love, friendships, sacrifice, and doing good for others. However, when they are unhealthy, they can use the church to boost their ego—projecting an image to others of being a savior figure or rescuer.[2]

While many Christians experience faith as an individualistic opportunity to consume religious content, Twos see the church the same way the apostle Paul did when he used "the body" as His primary metaphor, reminding us that "we were all baptized into one body."[3] In other words, when we become Christians, we are grafted into something bigger than ourselves. In such an individualistic world, you help us see the bigger picture—that connectedness implies responsibility. Ignoring or mistreating individuals will negatively affect the entire body because we are fundamentally *one*: "If one member suffers, all suffer together."[4] We all have the responsibility of loving one another as much as we love ourselves.

Perhaps the perfect metaphor for the Helpers' incredible contribution to the church is *the heart*, which is considered a vital organ for the health and wellbeing of the whole body. The heart is a muscle of astonishing strength at the center of your circulation system, which consists of an intricate weave of vessels and capillaries, extending throughout the body, carrying oxygen, nutrients, and healing antibodies to and from our hearts into every cell in our bodies. Just as the heart sends oxygen to the brain to help us think, or to the lungs to help us run, your life-giving support is like oxygen to our souls. Spiritually-speaking, our heart is the symbol of love, the perfect description of who you are to us. The heart also represents feeling-wisdom as opposed to head-wisdom, which describes the Twos ability to help us "get out of our heads" and lead with understanding and compassion.

Twos are the modern-day good Samaritans who don't overlook suffering people but stop everything they are doing to help others, no matter their nationality,

---

2   Riso and Hudson, *Personality Types*, 73.

3   1 Corinthians 12:13

4   1 Corinthians 12:26

religion, or social status.[5] They stay by people's sides through thick and thin and "bear one another's burdens, and so fulfill the law of Christ."[6] While some pastors and leaders are busy writing theological position papers or revising strategic plans, Twos are busy creating culture. As it's been said, "culture eats strategy for breakfast."[7]

The Good News for Helpers is although you may experience many relational ups and downs in the local church, remember that Christ holds all of us together.[8] We have a good *head* on our shoulders. And He sees all you do for the rest of the body. As Jesus says, "Truly, I say to you, as you did it to one of the least of these my brothers, you did it to me."[9] That means *every* gift, word of encouragement, act of service, and minute of time you spend with someone else in need is deeply felt, appreciated, and acknowledged by the King—whether it is done in public or private.[10]

→ Pray

Father, the intricate design of our human bodies points us to ascribe praise to a wonderful Creator. Thank You for arranging Your church in the same way and giving equal value to every part. Forgive us for our independence that keeps us from leaning on other parts of the body. Use me to help the church grow and be built up in love.[11]

---

5   Luke 10:25-37

6   Galatians 6:2

7   This quote has been attributed to management consultant and author Peter Drucker.

8   Colossians 1:17

9   Matthew 25:40

10   While Social Twos often gravitate toward more visible roles, many Twos are perfectly happy to serve behind the scenes.

11   Ephesians 4:16

Day 38 Reflections:

How has an individualistic mindset negatively affected our culture and churches? How does the metaphor of "the body" challenge this mindset?

What about the physical and spiritual understanding of the human heart provides clarity on your unique contribution to the church?

Where do you need to "show up" and help your local church next?

→ Respond

Identify an area of the church that is broken down, unsupported, or lacking in growth. Create a plan to build up that part of the body.

The Feedback Fugitive

The ear that listens to life-giving reproof will dwell among

the wise. Whoever ignores instruction despises himself,

but he who listens to reproof gains intelligence.

—Proverbs 15:31-32

WHAT'S YOUR FAVORITE FUGITIVE-SPY MOVIE? FROM JASON Bourne to James Bond, to the simply named *The Fugitive*, the plot-line is always the same but somehow they never fail to disappoint: the good guy (who everyone thinks is a bad guy) has to go on the run to escape arrest or avoid persecution. Throughout the film, this exceedingly smart and immensely capable now-fugitive deploys a variety of jaw-dropping tactics to mislead the frustrated authorities who, despite unlimited manpower and resources, are constantly one step behind. Ironically, this fictional storyline could be "based on a true story" if you consider the way Helpers seek to avoid being captured by negative feedback to avoid having their self-esteem deflated.

> Criticism, like rain, should be gentle enough to nourish a man's growth without destroying his roots.
>
> —Frank A. Clark

A Two's emotional sensitivity is one of their best strengths and is what makes them such a good friend or partner. However, when the strength is overdone, their feelings may lead them to perceive ill-will or rejection that isn't really there. They may take things personally even when they aren't personal. If you say, "I don't like your [x, y, or z]," they may hear, "I don't like *you*." Twos may know in their heads it's really not personal, but it sure feels that way! While criticism is hard for everyone, it is especially crushing for Twos because they often base their happiness on how others feel about them.

Unhealthy Twos walk around with an inflated sense of who they are and what they can do for their community. If this elevated sense of self gets punctured by constructive criticism or worse, negative feedback, they may get down on themselves for not keeping up the positive image they try so hard to maintain and may spiral into depression.[1] Cron and Stabile share, "Remind yourself you're neither the best nor the worst. Just you."[2]

> Feedback doesn't describe who you are but who you can become.

Proverbs says that there is such a thing as life-giving reproof. That's right. Constructive criticism can lead to a more fulfilling life. The wise sage says that if you listen to criticism you'll make your home next to the wise, but if you flee from feedback you'll end up "despising" yourself. For the Two, this doesn't just mean receiving constructive feedback, but quite surprisingly, it includes *positive* reinforcement as well.

In Suzanne Stabile's *The Path Between Us*, Hunter shares just how hard it is for a Two to receive positive affirmation:

> "It's very difficult to know who I am when I'm alone. I want responses from other people that show that they appreciate me, but I don't want to ask for them, and if I do receive accolades from others I have no idea how to handle them. So the most complicated time of my work week as a pastor is about twenty minutes after I've preached a sermon. After the service, I desperately want a line to form and to hear people say, 'That

---

1   Chestnut, *The 9 Types of Leadership*, 84.

2   Cron and Stabile, *The Road Back to You*, 128.

was the best sermon I've ever heard,' but when I do hear that I can't trust it. So, I wouldn't say I actually enjoy it. It's like something I need that I am not able to savor. I need people to affirm me and my work, but I can't receive it so I've learned to deflect it. I simply redirect the conversation so it's about the other person and not about me."[3]

The Good News for Helpers is that God already sees you clearly. No amount of hiding from negative or deflecting positive feedback will obscure the bright and beautiful aspects of who you are, nor the darker aspects as well. It's true that feedback comes in many forms. Whether these words of correction come in the harsh hail of attacks or the gentle rain of constructive feedback, you can choose to hear the words as enemies or as God-given gifts and opportunities for growth. The roots of your identity are in Christ—you won't be destroyed. Feedback doesn't describe who you are but who you can become. With the gospel in view, you will be able to invert the "fugitive" plot line and welcome those with feedback as the heroes in your life rather than the villains.

> ## → Pray
>
> Father, thank You for sending Your Son, Jesus, to dwell among us, full of grace and truth. If I claim to be good with no need of feedback, the truth is not in me. Because I am found in You, I don't have to fear being shamed because my status is secure. Help me speak the truth in love to others, valuing their spiritual growth over getting their approval.

---

3 Stabile, *The Path Between Us*, 78.

Day 39 Reflections:

How do you run from receiving or giving negative feedback? What are you afraid of?

Why do you deflect positive feedback? Is it because you don't believe it or don't want to appear as if you need it?

What are some hurtful words you've received that you can't get out of your head? Bring those to a loving God for healing.[4]

> ## → Respond
>
> Twos may struggle with downplaying praise because it feels too prideful to accept it. When someone compliments you this week, rather than deflecting, humbly receive it and tell them it was a needed gift.

---

4   Eddy, *Enneagram for Beginners*, 53.

The Next Chapter

For we are his workmanship, created in Christ Jesus for good works,

which God prepared beforehand, that we should walk in them.

—Ephesians 2:10

WHEN YOU LET YOURSELF THINK ABOUT THE next decade, what does it look like? Or are you so exhausted by all the things that need done today you can't think about the future? It's difficult for the average Helper to plan ahead. There's just so much that needs your attention! So let me ask an important question: *What would you do if everyone's needs were already met?*

> God calls you to the place where your deep gladness and the world's deep hunger meet.
>
> —Frederick Buechner[1]

Your ongoing mission must be to figure out what you *want* to be doing, not what you think you *should* be doing for others. Twos may get to the end of their lives with the realization that they were only doing what they (or others) thought they should be doing. You may find out too late that you chose a career that made

---

1 Frederick Buechner, *Wishful Thinking: A Theological ABC* (London, Mowbray, 1994), 119.

you feel more loved or needed. So let me ask you: Are you doing what you want? The needs you feel called to today may not be your long-term calling.

Being asked to do so many things for so many people will leave you stuck on a treadmill—always running but never feeling like you are going anywhere. When you care for everyone, you won't be able to care about the next "work" God has prepared for you. Therefore, you must learn to let go of the urge for the urgent and listen to God's specific calling.

Princess Diana, whose life ended far too early in a car accident at the age of thirty-six, was a shining example for all Twos. As a shy twenty-year-old woman, she became engaged to Prince Charles of Wales. She quickly emerged from the shadows of her husband into the national spotlight, becoming the "people's princess." Her single-minded mission was driven by this: "Everyone needs to be valued. Everyone has the potential to give something back if only they had the chance."[2] She worked to remove the stigma around HIV/AIDS, helped the young and homeless, and advocated for awareness of leprosy. Because of her work to alleviate suffering, it was said that "She will never be the queen of England, but she will be the queen of our hearts."[3] Though she wasn't a "princess" in the eyes of everyone because she spoke her mind and sometimes broke royal protocol, Diana taught us how to pursue big dreams, scheduling *her* priorities rather than letting her schedule (or critics) control her.

> What would you do if everyone's needs were already met?

Jesus is the supreme example of a Helper living on purpose, often saying no to urgent needs so He could prioritize the most important thing—getting to Jerusalem—to help the *most* people. Rather than staying in one town to heal, feed, or teach every person who asked, He often denied those wishes and fled. That was because the good works He accomplished were not His true task but stopping points on the way to Jerusalem, where He would do the main work that had been prepared for Him by the Father. Think of that: seeing people who need

---

2   "Achievements of Princess Diana," Biography Online, March 6, 2019, https://www.biographyonline.net/people/diana/achievements_princess_diana.html.

3   Ibid.

help and knowing you could help them but choosing to step away from their needs to focus on your calling.

You too can show up in the world with your authentic self and a defined purpose that is confident and unbending. Listen closely, you are more than someone's helper (even if the Enneagram says you are!); you are more than a spouse; you are more than a parent; you are more than your church's lead volunteer; you are more than someone's best friend; you are more than the star employee at your boss's beck and call.

The Good News for Helpers is that you are God's masterpiece, and He has already written a beautiful story for you to play a leading role in. Don't be tempted to take yourself out of your own headline; you were not created to be the supporting cast in your own story. It's time to move from being a "go-to" person for others to becoming your *own* person.

What big goal or dream has God placed on your heart? As we come to the end of our 40-day journey, remember that God is crazy about you––He loves you apart from what you do for others. He doesn't need you but wants you. As your best friend, He'll never stop pursuing you, thinking about your needs, or anticipating what exciting thing He'll get to do with you next.

→ Pray

Father, I know You believe in me because I am Your beloved child, created with a purpose. Help me believe in myself. I know if I abide in You, I can ask whatever I wish and it will be done for me.[4] So I'm asking nothing less than for You to change the world through me. Use me as a main character in Your unfolding plan to reconcile all things.

---

4   John 15:7

Day 40 Reflections:

Where do you sense God leading you to in the next chapter of your life?

How do you want the world to remember you?

What are your biggest takeaways from the last 40 days?

→ Respond

Find a life coach or spiritual mentor to come alongside and support you in accomplishing your goals. Start working courageously toward something today that seems impossible without God's supernatural power and grace.

Father, I am deeply grateful to You for creating me in Your image as Your beloved child. You created me to specifically reflect Your love and care. I confess that the weight of responsibility I feel for others has often left me feeling exhausted and underappreciated. I have found myself at times being flattering, passive-aggressive, martyr-like, and intrusive. You, being rich in mercy, saw me from heaven and sent Your selfless Son, Jesus, to die on the cross when I was needy and helpless. Now, I revel in the fact that You want me, rescued me, and will never reject me. Clothed with the power of the Holy Spirit, I will view love not only as what I can give but also what I can receive, trusting that the Holy Spirit will help everyone I can't. Putting off pride and putting on my new, humble self made in Christ's image, I will pursue self-care over self-forgetfulness, God pleasing over people pleasing, and boundaries over codependency, knowing I don't have to be needed to be perfectly loved.

Three Types of Helpers

BELOW IS A SUMMARY OF THE THREE types of Twos (called subtypes) from the teaching of Beatrice Chestnut, whose book, *The Complete Enneagram* covers all twenty-seven subtypes of the main nine Enneagram types.[1] As discussed in the introduction, these subtypes are helpful in drilling down the different nuances of the Helper.

Warning: many of these descriptions will seem overly negative. However, one of the main purposes of the Enneagram is to help us discover our "shadow self"— the ways we interact with the world unconsciously and often in times of stress. These descriptions are not indictments; rather, they are a further opportunity to deepen our awareness of how to interact with the world.

The Self-Preservation Two

The Self-Preservation Two, often the teacher's pet growing up, has a playful personality, and often unconsciously leverages their "youthful" sweetness and charm to gain affection and get others to take care of them. Just like a beloved child, they want to receive attention and love not for what they do, but for who they are. They also maintain a childlike posture to evoke care from others without having to ask for it. Being more sensitive, their feelings get hurt easily by criticism or disapproval and may result in tantrums or sulking. They long for freedom but may end up becoming too dependent on others to avoid responsibility, resulting in them giving away too much of their power. This Two is the "countertype" because they are more fearful and less trusting than other Twos, which can lead to relational ambivalence. The difference between the Self-Preservation Two and its most similar subtype, the Self-Preservation Six, is that the Six's fear is generalized, while this Two's fear primarily manifests in relationships. Aside from Sixes, this subtype can also be mistyped as a Four because they are romantic and express more emotionality but repress their needs and true feelings more than an authentic Four.

---

1 Chestnut, *The Complete Enneagram*.

The Social Two

Whereas the Self-Preservation Two "gets low'" and leverages their childlike charm to get what they want, the adultlike Social Two seeks to be "on top" to cultivate an image of being an influential person who holds power and authority. They may work at a high level in their organization or be a leader in their field. These ambitious Twos are seducers of environments who are good in front of groups, seeking to impress others by being exceptional and intellectual. Although it often happens on an unconscious level, the Social Two seeks to gain the favor of important people, relying on strategic giving as a way of securing allegiance and respect. They can often resemble a Three, becoming goal-oriented, competitive, and successful or a workaholic. Social Twos can also be mistyped as Eights because they may engage in power struggles, become territorial, or want to dominate as the powerful protector. However, unlike both Threes and Eights, Twos have a softer presence and can more readily access their emotions and be vulnerable on the way to their goals.

The One-to-One Two

Whereas Social Twos seduce environments, the One-to-One Two woos specific individuals as a way of getting their needs met. Similar to the "femme fatale" archetype (and male equivalent), this Two uses their charm, sexuality, and generosity to secure a strong bond with an ideal partner who will provide an endless supply of love, favors, and other gifts. Thus, this Two is more of a "lover" than a "helper" or "giver." Humorously, this subtype has been associated with the "dangerous beauty" of a vampire: consuming another person with their engulfing love. This Two seeks to become irresistible, inspiring others with their passion and positive feelings to get what they want. Unlike the Self-Preservation Two, this subtype is more aggressive, doing what they please when they please, not asking but taking. Though this is the most "classic" Two, they can sometimes be confused with One-to-One Threes and One-to-One Fours who also focus on being attractive. However, the big difference is that Threes are focused on outward success, Fours on their own inner-world, and Twos on getting their emotional needs met through others.

Next Steps

I'm so proud of you for finishing this 40-day journey. That's a big accomplishment! Though this book isn't small by any means, you may feel (like me) that we've only begun to explore the tip of the iceberg. You're probably wondering: *What now? My eyes have been opened, I've grown in greater self-awareness and empathy, and now I'm ready to take the next step!* Here are some ideas:

1. Follow "Gospel for Enneagram" on Instagram, YouTube, Facebook, or Twitter to continue learning and engaging.

2. Download my free resource called *Should Christians Use The Enneagram?* at gospelforenneagram.com.

3. If you found this book helpful, please leave an honest review (or star rating) online or share on social media so others can find it.

4. Visit my website, gospelforenneagram.com, to find more helpful links and resources.

5. Join a church community where you can continue to grow in your knowledge of God and self. To go the distance, find a mentor, coach, or support system.

6. Ask a friend, spouse, or mentor to meet regularly with you to discuss the insights God has revealed to you through this book. Invite them, along with your small group, t o get a devotional on their Enneagram type and share what they learn with you.

7. Email me with any thoughts, questions, or feedback to tyler@gospelforenneagram.com. I'd love to hear from you!

Acknowledgements

My wife: Lindsey, you show me the gospel every day by loving me for who I am and not what I do. Thank you for your tremendous encouragement to be a writer and for bearing with my workaholic tendencies. I want to be more like you.

My editors: Joshua, thank you for bringing your incredible creativity to the table. Your re-rewrites helped elevate my writing to a whole new level. Stephanie, because you are a Two, I appreciate that you took your time through this book, offering a tremendous amount of encouragement along the way. Your helpful comments made this book so much better than what it would have been. Thank you for Lee Ann, your veteran experience and thoroughness increased the value of this book tremendously.

My coach: John Fooshee, thank you for your Enneagram coaching and partnership. I'm deeply grateful for your willingness to come alongside me and put wind in my sails.

My influences: I wouldn't have been able to pull this off without a multitude of direct and indirect influences such as pastors, teachers, and writers (including you, mom!) over the years. I'm deeply grateful for the spiritual heroes that have come before me and shaped me..

www.GospelForEnneagram.com

Follow us:

 /GospelForEnneagram

 @GospelForEnneagram

 @GospelForGram

 Gospel For Enneagram